EARLY CHILDHOOD EDUCATION SERIES
Leslie R. Williams, Editor

(continued)

Guiding Children's Behavior

DEVELOPMENTAL DISCIPLINE IN THE CLASSROOM

EILEEN S. FLICKER

JANET ANDRON HOFFMAN

Foreword by Leslie R. Williams

Teachers College, Columbia University
New York and London

Published by Teachers College Press, 1234 Amsterdam Avenue, New York, NY 10027

Library of Congress Cataloging-in-Publication Data

Flicker, Eileen S.
    Guiding children's behavior : developmental discipline in the classroom / Eileen S. Flicker, Janet Andron Hoffman.
        p. cm.—(Early childhood education series)
    Includes bibliographical references and index.
    ISBN-13: 978-0-8077-4713-1 (pbk. : alk. paper)
    ISBN-10: 0-8077-4713-0 (pbk. : alk. paper)
    1. School discipline—United States.   2. Behavior modification.   I. Hoffman, Janet Andron.
II. Title.   III. Series: Early childhood education series (Teachers College Press)
    LB3012.2.F55   2006
    371.5—dc22   2006010061

ISBN-13: 978-0-8077-4713-1 (paper)   ISBN-10: 0-8077-4713-0 (paper)

Printed on acid-free paper
Manufactured in the United States of America

13 12 11 10 09 08 07 06   8 7 6 5 4 3 2 1

To our children,

Marti, **Max**, **Sam**, **Hannah**, **Yardena**, **Dave**, **Ilan**, **Ariel**, and **Zorro**,

who supplied us with endless opportunities to practice developmental discipline.

Contents

Foreword

Few aspects of teaching are as worrisome to novice teachers as that of children's "behavior." Haunted by memories of the substitute teacher who struggled in vain to control the rowdy and unsympathetic 4th graders who were torturing her, these teachers-to-be remember that even they (the "good" children in the class) had not rescued her. Surely their time of retribution is coming as they enter their first year of full-time teaching. And contrary to their expectations, their ongoing teacher preparation has not magically resolved their fears. Few of their courses or field experiences have directly addressed their concerns about losing control of the classroom.

Nor is it novice teachers alone who are consumed with such doubts. Even highly experienced teachers are aware that working with children entails a continual balancing act between the aims of children and their own aims as teachers, as each attempts to use the power of the moment to best advantage. Children wish to satisfy their urge to learn and to grow beyond present capability. Teachers wish to have the satisfaction of success in their teaching, to know that they have made a difference in the development of the children in their care. What resources might teachers find to strengthen their intent and hone the skills needed to channel the energies of learning to best effect for all involved?

Happily for both groups of teachers and all those in between, Eileen Flicker and Janet Hoffman's *Guiding Children's Behavior: Developmental Discipline in the Classroom* offers both the theory and the practice to yield such results. Strongly rooted in recognition of the importance of the early childhood

years, the authors illustrate many of the ways that children from infancy through the elementary school years may challenge their teachers' expectations for constructive and productive classroom behavior. Their first premise is a straightforward one—behaviors of all varieties are learned in the context of the sociocultural environments in which children are embedded. To each encounter, children bring with them their past observations and experiences and are sensitive to the responses modeled by those in authority around them. In order for children to develop positive and affirming ways of treating themselves and others, their teachers must think through and anticipate the consequences of their own actions. All such reflection must be built conscientiously on their observations of children's behaviors, knowledge of child development, and awareness of the children's (and their own) cultural patterns of initiation and response in situations of stressful exchange.

To maintain this high level of awareness on which to base effective action, teachers must value and invite interaction with families, to learn from them at the same time as they share their perspectives as educators. They must develop links with the ethos of the communities within which they work in order to understand the meanings of particular behaviors and the power those behaviors hold for the children themselves. Nothing about this approach to classroom behavior is formulaic. It is envisioned as an active response to a highly dynamic situation—the condition of living fully in each moment of exchange with children, engaging with the present while recognizing its connection to both the past and the future.

A distinctive feature of Flicker and Hoffman's work is their articulation of all aspects of *Guiding Children's Behavior* with their vision of curriculum. They never lose sight of their second premise—that the purpose of guiding behavior in constructive ways in classrooms is to facilitate learning. The corollary to that connection is that the domain of knowledge and skills is at the heart of schooling. The functions of the mind are intended to be refined in the school, and that can happen only if all concerned—children, teachers, and families —demonstrate behaviors that support learning. Thus, an important connection is established and maintained in this approach to behavior. Classroom discipline is not a thing in itself. It is not advocated for its own sake, but as a path to growth in knowledge and skills.

The authors make their position clear through use of vignettes that illustrate moments when learning could proceed or be subverted. The text abounds with descriptions that even novice teachers will recognize as all-too-common events that threaten children's learning as children interfere with one another's work, exclude particular children from engagement, or sabotage their own growth by creating conditions that work against their learning. The authors also include abundant examples of ways that teachers may themselves set barriers to children's learning in order to assert authority at the expense of a particular child or a group of children. They also provide thoughtful analyses of these instances to illustrate how reflection can open new paths for action in ways that honor the needs of children and recognize the children's strengths; and they include a variety of tools that can be used either as they are or adapted to particular circumstances to support problem-solving in the alignment of behaviors toward promotion of learning. These concrete suggestions are bound to be helpful not only to novices reading this book, but also to experienced teachers who wish to reformulate their practice.

In their concluding chapters, Flicker and Hoffman point out that, in order to reach the full benefit of developmental discipline, it requires investment of time and energy. Commitment to the approach requires not only allegiance to the concepts behind it, but rehearsal of the skills involved within a like-minded community of educators. This is a caution that experienced teachers will understand well, as they have in their careers undoubtedly seen many instances of how intention alone can be swept away by lack of concentrated action. This book provides a resource needed by those experienced teachers, as well as by novices, to actualize the vision of constructive connection that permeates the work. I think you may agree that the investment of such energy will be well spent.

—Leslie R. Williams, Ed.D.
Professor of Education,
Teachers College, Columbia University

Acknowledgments

We would first like to thank Dr. Leslie R. Williams of Teachers College, Columbia University, for her steadfast and supportive role in our professional lives. Leslie showed us how to be effective educators by always focusing on the positive and by stressing the importance of nurturing students. We have been blessed by Leslie's mentorship and this book is the result of her enduring influence on our practice. Leslie's editorial expertise was invaluable.

Thank you also to our editors, Susan Liddicoat, Marie Ellen Larcada, and Karl Nyberg, for their thoughtful comments and thoroughness, and for guiding us through the world of publishing.

We are indebted to our parents for encouraging us to climb the next mountain, whether personal or professional. They enabled us to pursue our interests and to accomplish our dreams.

Our husbands, Lee and Kenny, deserve a special thanks for their ongoing support throughout this arduous process. We appreciate their love, patience, and good humor. Without them, this project could never have been completed.

We are most grateful to the many teachers and administrators who welcomed us into their classrooms and shared their insights and observations.

Finally, we thank the hundreds of children and families who inspired us with their ordinary and unique challenges. We remain committed to working collaboratively with them.

Introduction

Fighting, cursing, disrespect, outbursts, and destruction—these and other behavioral problems have plagued schools. Even experienced teachers find classroom management to be a daunting challenge. Children have expressed both resentment and fear of disruptive behavior from their peers. As educational and mental health consultants, we have observed children out of control in early childhood and elementary schools, in classrooms, hallways, lunchrooms, assemblies, recess, and specials.

Guiding Children's Behavior: Developmental Discipline in the Classroom is written for teachers and administrators addressing challenging behavior in young children. Developmental discipline emphasizes observations and insights as a guide to intervention. This approach is not a set of isolated strategies to specific disciplinary problems, but rather a system through which teachers help children to monitor behavior and to understand the ramifications of their actions. At the same time, teachers assess their own curriculum, pedagogical style, and quality of communications with students to determine the effectiveness of their practice. The adult and child are partners in a disciplinary process in which they reflect on the nature of behavior. Sensitivity to the child's individual temperament, communications, and needs is necessary to achieve a harmonious dynamic. Weaving cultural awareness into observations and interactions enhances understanding and improves relationships.

Problematic behavior at school is not a new phenomenon. However, the degree and complexity of inappropriate behavior, which disrupts classroom learning, has demanded more attention in recent years. Cotton (2000) suggests that about one half of all classroom time is spent, not on instruction, but rather on discipline problems and transitions. Even experienced teachers have observed the deterioration of conduct in their classrooms. A study conducted by the California Department of Education in 1992 (Collins & Frantz, 1993) compared disciplinary problems in schools in the 1940s and 1980s. The results reveal that in the 1940s teachers focused on issues such as getting children to stay in line and throw out their trash. By the 1980s, however, teachers were dealing with drug use, aggression, stealing, and promiscuity. Garbarino (1995), when discussing raising children in a toxic society, noted a similar trend when querying educators who had been teaching since the 1950s. Teachers reported that in the 1950s children were reprimanded for "gum chewing, talking back, disorder in the hallways, making a mess in the classroom, dress-code violations and being noisy" (p. 1). More recently, teachers experience similar antisocial acts to those that were cited in the California Department of Education study. While such behaviors are more commonly found in middle and high school students, most experts agree that even in elementary school, classroom management poses bigger challenges today than in the past (Willis, 1996). A variety of societal changes that affect both families and schools have reduced the effectiveness of traditional classroom management strategies.

HISTORICAL PERSPECTIVES

Reviewing how children's behavior was perceived in the past helps us understand how we have evolved to this point. Children's behavior and adults' responses have always been predicated by the sociological, philosophical, and psychological influences of the day. Schools too are a reflection of these societal trends. Both teachers and children are a product of their own upbringing, cultural background, and disciplinary practices, and these dynamics are often played out in the school setting.

In American history, society has witnessed the swinging of the pendulum from punitive discipline to a more permissive model. The use of strict discipline to control children's behavior, an offshoot of Calvinist belief, was evident in the 1600s during the time of the Puritans. Religious leaders espoused obedience and an unwavering adherence to rules. New England schools reinforced a stern approach by demanding respect for teachers and good manners. Teachers would regularly slap and spank children with birch rods, cat-o'-nine-tails, and paddles to maintain order in the classroom (Bossard & Boll, 1966).

In the early 1900s there was a continuation of the use of punishment at home and in schools to build character. The behaviorist theory of J. B. Watson recommended a strict scheduling of routines and minimal expression of affection toward children to ensure obedience and develop character. The obedience model (Curwin & Mendler, 1999) was characterized by absolute compliance to rules without consideration of children's perspectives. Punishment was used to inhibit children's natural impulses. This model was in direct contrast to the teachings of the Child Study Association of America, based on the work of Sigmund Freud and G. S. Hall, which advocated permissiveness and a more nurturing style of interaction (Berger, 2000).

The child guidance movement (Gartrell, 2004), based on the work of Johann Heinrich Pestalozzi, Friedrich Froebel, Maria Montessori, and John Dewey, was a child-centered approach to discipline. Children's developmental readiness was incorporated into teachers' practice. The emphasis was on children's self-control rather than on externally imposed discipline.

By the mid 1940s, parents were influenced by Dr. Benjamin Spock, who promoted a balanced, "firm and friendly" approach to discipline (Spock & Rothenberg, 1985, p. 401). Spock discouraged parents from spanking their children, believing that it made children resentful and inadvertently led to more violent behavior. Ginott's work (1965) continued in this vein by encouraging parents to talk about feelings and discipline in a positive manner. Similarly, Ginott (1972) encouraged teachers to consider alternatives to punishment that would foster children's self-esteem. He believed that punishment made children more "careful, not more honest and responsible" (p. 151).

The logical consequence approach was proposed by Dreikurs and Grey (1968), who stated that children should be given choices rather than be forced to comply with teacher-imposed directives. These authors were proponents of a democratic classroom system in which students play an active role in determining rules. A good relationship between teachers and pupils is an essential ingredient in these classrooms to emphasize children's acceptance of their mistakes as they experience the logical consequences of their actions.

The "parent effectiveness training" model of the 1970s (Gordon, 1970) endorsed "active listening," whereby parents reflect their children's feelings back to them. Both verbal and nonverbal expressions demonstrate that parents are genuinely listening. Gordon advocated the use of "I messages" to help parents communicate with their children. I messages consist of three parts: how the parents feel, a description of the problematic behavior, and a statement of why this behavior is so upsetting to the parents. Parents were encouraged to pay attention to their own feelings and to provide a forum for constructive communication so that both positive and negative feelings could be shared. Gordon (1976) extended this model to include a teacher effectiveness training program that stressed a child's ownership of the problem, environmental modifications to change behavior, and active listening between teacher and student.

Assertive discipline, an alternative model designed by Lee Canter in the late 1970s, uses behavior modification and encourages teachers to be clear and decisive in their establishment of rules and expectations. Being an assertive teacher requires being firm, being straightforward in expressing desires and feelings, and following through on words with actions if necessary

(Edwards, 2004). A system of positive consequences as a reward for desired behavior is used.

CURRENT TRENDS

Currently, there are two contrasting styles of discipline in American society, reflecting both past and present child-rearing philosophies. Child development specialists almost unanimously oppose corporal punishment and instead endorse positive methods to teach children right from wrong (e.g., Balter, 1985; Brazelton, 1992; Hyman, 1997; Nelson, Erwin, & Duffy, 1995; Wyckoff & Unell, 1984). These experts recommend discipline through discussion, explanation, limit setting, and enforcing consequences instead of intimidation or physical force.

At the same time, many parents (and educators as well) use physical punishment to control behavior. As early as the 1800s, corporal punishment was seen as the routine method of discipline in schools, stemming from the belief that "to spare the rod was to spoil the child." "Paddling of recalcitrant children has long been an accepted method of promoting good behavior and instilling notions of responsibility and decorum into the mischievous hearts of school children" (Greven, 1992, p. 102). Only two states, Massachusetts and New York, prohibited this form of discipline in public schools prior to 1977. In that year a landmark decision by the Supreme Court (*Ingraham v. Wright*), upheld the right for both teachers and administrators to discipline by physical means within the public schools, providing that this force was "reasonable." It was not until March 1990 that 20 additional states prohibited corporal punishment in schools. Kohn (1999) reports that corporal punishment in public schools is still permitted in most of the United States, though long abandoned in most developed nations. However, many teachers rely on a reward-and-punishment system to manage behavior in the classroom. Rewards might include stickers, pizza parties, and "no homework" passes. Time-out, loss of recess, and removal from the classroom are standard practices to punish children in school.

Discipline practices in our society appear to lean toward the extremes: adults being overly punitive or excessively lenient. Parents and teachers often lack a middle ground, or what Baumrind (1991) calls an authoritative discipline style. Baumrind describes three broad categories of parenting styles, which relate to teaching styles as well. Authoritarian parents enforce rules with harsh, punitive discipline. They have low tolerance for children's misbehavior and offer little nurturance, warmth, or affection. Permissive parents discipline either inconsistently or not at all. Baumrind further separates permissive parents into two distinct patterns: indulgent and neglectful. Indulgent parents exhibit a high level of warmth and affection while at the same time giving in to their child's every whim. Neglectful parents, by contrast, are emotionally uninvolved and express little interest in their child's behavior. Finally, authoritative disciplinarians provide a warm and loving environment while still maintaining clear limits and high expectations. Dreikurs and Grey (1968) apply a similar conceptualization to teachers: an autocratic style, whereby teachers exercise a firm control of the classroom without input from the students; permissiveness, in which there is a lack of enforced rules; and a democratic approach, which gives the students a voice in the classroom and encourages student accountability.

Baumrind (1967) discovered that children raised in permissive homes were found to be aggressive, impulsive, noncompliant, and lacking in self-control. Children raised in authoritarian environments tended to be aggressive, moody, and easily annoyed. Children raised in authoritative homes, however, were more self-reliant, self-controlled, and cooperative with adults and better able to cope with stress. We suggest that excessive, inconsistent, or nonexistent discipline at home contributes in part to the deterioration of classroom behavior.

It seems that a permissive child-rearing atmosphere is a particularly harmful environment for young children because without limits and guidelines children feel insecure and scared. While children may insist on having their own way and may seem happy when they initially get it, they are really crying out for boundaries, which create a sense of safety and security. Without consistent discipline, they typically act out to get those very limits that have been denied them. One may not be overly concerned with the toddler who has frequent temper tantrums or refuses to go to sleep. However, without timely and thoughtful intervention, negative behaviors in young children may continue and escalate into more inappropriate and destructive patterns of behavior. Ehrensaft, in her *Spoiling Childhood* (1997), emphasizes that middle-class parents are overly indulgent and unwilling to say no. "Parents offer friendship instead of guidance. They treat their children like princes and princesses and prime them for success even before they exit the birth canal" (p. 3). This lenient style may be more predominant in today's generation of parents, who are rebelling against their own parents' authoritarian approach (Cummings, 2000).

SOCIAL CHANGES

In addition to child-rearing styles, there have been changes in the nuclear family itself that have resulted in difficulties in raising and disciplining children and subsequently in classroom management. Only one in four families consists of a married couple living with their children (Washington & Andrews, 1998). According to the *State of America's Children Yearbook* (Children's Defense Fund, 2001), one in every two children will live in a single-parent family at some point during childhood. Additionally, there are currently 5.4 million children living in households headed by relatives other than their own parent. Children living with only one adult are six times as likely to be poor (Whitehead, 1993). Nearly one in five children (18.9%) lives in poverty; this percentage is doubled for Blacks and Hispanics (Gestwicki, 2000).

Poverty, homelessness, substance abuse, and family violence are all factors that increase stress in adults trying to parent effectively. Garbarino (1995) identifies these forces as socially "toxic" for children. Children living under such conditions are more vulnerable in their overall development and are more likely to exhibit problematic behavior in the classroom. Payne (1998) associates poverty with disrespect, arguing, anger, vulgarity, and verbal and physical abuse. She further asserts that given the high incidence of poverty in the United States, more than 25% of students manifest these behaviors in the classroom. Contrary to what many might believe, affluence is not necessarily a safeguard against family dysfunction and behavioral difficulties in school. Substance abuse and domestic violence are equally prevalent in middle- and upper-middle-class families (Springate & Stegelin, 1999).

The advent of women in the workforce has also altered the nature of child rearing. As of 1998, 65.2% of mothers with children under the age of 6 and 70% of mothers with school-age children were in the workforce (Washington & Andrews, 1998). Children of working parents are often inadequately disciplined because working parents have less time and energy to devote to their children. Stressed and exhausted parents are not necessarily thinking about the long term but rather surviving another day, and they may subsequently pay a price for not enforcing rules. Furthermore, caregivers may not be reinforcing parents' rules either. Children suffer from not having clear, firm, and consistent limits and are more at risk in their development.

Another precipitating factor in the increase of behavior problems in schools is children's regular exposure to violence and provocative themes in television, movies, video and computer games, and the news. It is estimated that 67% of households with children own a video game system (Subrahmanyam, Kraut, Greenfield, & Gross, 2001). Furthermore, nearly two-thirds of video games rated "E for Everyone" include intentional violence where injuring or killing characters is rewarded or required for advancement in the game (Thompson, 2001). The number of violent acts embedded in children's television programming is steadily increasing, along with the degree to which these images are portrayed realistically (Levin, 2003). Longitudinal research has found that by the time children reach adolescence, they view 18,000 acts of television violence (Curwin & Mendler, 1999). Research further indicates that watching violent imagery increases the likelihood of aggressive behavior in children (Bandura, 1963; Children's Defense Fund, 2001; Kaiser & Rasminsky, 1999; National Association for the Education of Young Children, 1990). Steyer (2002) suggests that when children watch an excessive amount of television, the media becomes the "other parent." The media's influence is then insidious.

Overcrowded classes and inadequate support systems for the increasing behavior problems in our schools further tests teachers and administrators. Additionally, the pedagogical and political shift from tracking to heterogeneous grouping and inclusion makes teaching all the more difficult. Meeting the needs of children from various cultures presents unique challenges. Cultural differences in expectations, values, and language can sometimes create misunderstandings between children, or between children and teachers. Assumptions are made based on one's worldview, and differences in perspectives yield dissimilar interpretations of the same situation (Campbell & Smith, 2001). Teachers' values, which may be related to culture and socioeconomic status, may inevitably influence expectations for children's behavior. *Guiding Children's Behavior: Developmental Discipline in the Classroom* will help educators look beyond the specific behavior to understand the child within the context of the school, family, and society.

GOALS OF DEVELOPMENTAL DISCIPLINE

An overall goal of developmental discipline is for teachers to better understand the reasons for children's misbehavior in order to guide them sensitively and effectively. Specific goals include:

- Enhancing the classroom learning environment
- Strengthening the classroom community through improved social interactions
- Helping teachers to recognize and be sensitive to diverse cultural patterns of behavior
- Reducing stress in children and teachers by building coping skills
- Fine-tuning teachers' observational skills and encouraging them to reflect on their practice and consider the following:

    —Why is this child acting out?
    —Are my responses effective?
    —What is the impact of my actions on the child and the entire class?
    —How does my curriculum influence behavior and the social/emotional climate of the classroom?

- Encouraging children to reflect and understand their own behavior
- Partnering with parents to provide continuity between home and school

Throughout this book, vignettes are used as a springboard for discussion about classroom behavior problems. Teachers will likely relate to these real-life situations and discover how developmental discipline can be implemented to address a variety of conflicts that arise in early childhood programs and elementary schools. There are no magical solutions for resolving classroom behavior problems. Observations alone do not simply give teachers answers, but rather provide clues. Reflective questioning along with systematic observations yield fresh perspectives on what teachers are seeing in their classrooms.

OVERVIEW OF THIS BOOK

In Chapter 1 we introduce the developmental discipline approach. The vignettes are used here to emphasize the importance of observation in effective discipline. Adults are asked to consider the various factors that cause children to act out or misbehave, including developmental, cultural, and environmental causes. Observations are the starting points for learning what the operative factors are and how to best respond to specific situations.

Using principles of developmental discipline, in Chapter 2 we encourage teachers to see children and curriculum as interrelated. Every child is viewed as an individual learner as well as a member of the classroom community. We emphasize the teacher's role in preventing and managing challenging behaviors through curricular changes within the social milieu.

Observation, the focus of Chapter 3, is an essential component of developmental discipline. Teachers and administrators observe children in the various environments within the school to learn more about the specific circumstances surrounding the misbehavior. The educator uses action research (Macintyre, 2000) to determine how best to respond. Self-reflection by students and adults is an integral part of this process.

In Chapter 4 we stress the importance of rules and limits in the early years. Developmental discipline starts in infancy with parents and teachers/caregivers developing positive behavior patterns. Parents often fall into the trap of not disciplining children early enough, to later be faced with the task of breaking bad habits. Typical daily caregiving routines are prime opportunities for parents and child-care providers to introduce limits to very young children. Adults are encouraged to look at the child's "negative" behaviors, such as their saying no or hitting, within the context of normal child development.

In Chapter 5 issues affecting the preschooler and kindergartner are addressed. Children between 3 and 5 years of age are confronted with many new experiences outside of the family setting. They must adapt to an environment filled with new adults and children and expectations different from those of home. Typical concerns that emerge during these years are discussed, and developmentally appropriate strategies are presented.

A discussion of common issues confronting school-age children and their influences on behavior is taken up in Chapter 6. Some of these concerns have plagued our youth throughout history and in all cultures while others are particular to our contemporary high-pressured society. Developmental discipline offers an approach to understanding children as they grapple with social, emotional, and physical changes.

In Chapter 7 we look at discipline methodologies that are frequently used in schools. Some of these practices are questioned in regard to their effectiveness. The practices include removing disruptive children from the classroom and eliminating recess as a response to negative or inappropriate behavior. Although it may seem appropriate to insist that children apologize for their misbehavior, there are consequences of this practice, and they are examined in Chapter 7. The importance of helping children feel and express genuine remorse is discussed. With its focus on observation of the individual child and the teacher's role, developmental discipline offers an alternative approach to discipline.

In the final chapter of the book we emphasize the importance of teachers, administrators, and parents working together to create more consistency between home and school. To that end, a developmental-discipline training module for faculty is presented. A menu of suggested strategies from which educators can draw is included.

CHAPTER 1

What Is Developmental Discipline?

Darryl and Anthony are 5-year-olds playing in the block area of their kindergarten classroom. For the most part they are working independently, although they occasionally talk to each other. Suddenly, both reach for the same block and begin to struggle. After a few moments of pulling and yelling, Anthony pulls back his arm as if to punch Darryl.

Teachers approach this situation in very different ways depending upon their experience, training, and belief systems. One might immediately intervene, either by separating the boys, putting Anthony in time-out, or taking away the desired block. Another would go to Anthony and encourage him to use his words. Still another teacher would watch closely to see if the boys resolved their dispute on their own. A teacher, at her wit's end, might even lose her temper and yell at the boys to stop fighting or else they would lose their recess.

These various responses, all of which are understandable, reflect in part the philosophies of the educator and school. However, they may result in very different outcomes depending on the fit between the child and the intervention. There are some children for whom time-out and reprimands are meaningless. They would either ignore the teacher's request, or would resume their scuffle once the teacher's back was turned or the time-out period was over. For other children, removing the

block or being removed from the block area might exacerbate the situation even further.

Teachers often intervene with the goal of stopping an inappropriate behavior while not considering the long-term ramifications of their actions. Children may cease fighting over the block out of fear of punishment or the adult's authority and not truly learn how to resolve their own conflicts. It is reasonable to expect a teacher, faced with children fighting over materials, to automatically respond if a child is being threatened with harm. Separating children, removing toys or learning materials, and using time-out are part of a teacher's repertoire for resolving classroom conflicts. Yet these strategies do not always work, because the consequence is not always related to the infraction, the individual child, and the unique set of circumstances. Furthermore, these commonly used disciplinary techniques do not help children regulate their own behavior in other situations when the adult is not present.

Ideally, the goal of discipline is for children to understand the ramifications of their actions and to develop self-control. The disciplinary process is only successful when children incorporate adults' rules into their own inner voices, which remind them what is acceptable and what is not. Children become cognizant of their effect on other people and situations when they clearly recognize consequences. They need to be allowed to naturally experience the impact of their behavior without being shielded from it. For example, a child who immediately is sent to the principal for destroying a classmate's diorama would not have the opportunity to witness his classmate's reaction or its impact on the class as a whole. While it is possible that he might have intended to cause a reaction, it is also possible that he was not aware of how devastated the other child would be or how disruptive his behavior actually was.

Natural consequences expose children to the direct outcome of their conduct. When children are encouraged to reflect on their actions and feelings, they become more in control of them; they develop a sense of ownership. This is critical in order for children to assume responsibility for their behavior. Logical consequences—a related concept—require an adult to make sensible and timely responses that specifically relate to the misbehavior (Browne, 2000). Here, the adult purposefully creates a situation that holds the child accountable. For example, a child who does not participate in the cleanup of art materials is prohibited from using them on the following day. In order to link children's misbehaviors with logical consequences, it is critical for teachers to use observation.

OBSERVATIONS—THE KEY TO UNDERSTANDING BEHAVIOR

Observation enables teachers to interpret children's behavior and intervene most effectively. When teachers understand the underlying motivations, they can respond in a way that best reaches children. Removing a privilege from a child who is acting out because she is depressed does not address the root of the problem. Merely acknowledging the manifest negative behavior will more than likely result in its repetition, because the latent situation has not been recognized.

Learning about children through observation is the basis of teaching and interacting. According to Seefeldt (1998), observation is "probably the oldest, most frequently used and most rewarding method of assessing children, their growth, development and learning" (p. 313). Genishi (1992) and Levine (1992), in his Schools Attuned approach, also emphasize the use of observation for assessing children and developing curriculum. Observation is the heart of teachers' work. It guides teachers' thinking, planning, and implementation. Teachers observe all the time. They observe children's interactions with one another, the content of their play and learning,

their questions and responses, and the choices they make. From these observations teachers infer children's individual learning styles, strengths, weaknesses, preferences, and needs. They also gain an understanding of children's functioning in all developmental domains, which should influence curricular decisions. Teachers also use observation to effectively deal with behavior; they watch, document, interpret, and then act. Both child assessment and the added component of teacher reflection are enhanced through ongoing and systematic observation.

Developmental discipline, an approach based on observation, helps teachers integrate their knowledge of child development with their understanding of the individual child and situation. Considering the child's developmental level (skills and comprehension) as well as recognizing his or her uniqueness is also paramount to effective discipline. With developmental discipline, teachers are scientists who collect objective information, reflect on those data, and then use them to intervene appropriately. This method is an extension of action research (e.g., Brennan & Noffke, 1998), in which teachers gather pertinent information on children to reflect on their teaching and disciplining. Observation is most beneficial when it engages children in the process.

THEORETICAL FOUNDATIONS

Developmental discipline draws upon the theories of Piaget (1929) and Vygotsky (1978), who believed that children are active participants in their cognitive and social/emotional development. Children are dynamically engaged in the acquisition of knowledge and are not just passive recipients of information from adults. Both Vygotsky and Piaget maintained that development is a gradual process and that mastery of skills and concepts occurs slowly over time. Experiences need to be repeated for knowledge and skills to be acquired and ultimately integrated into children's cognitive and behavioral framework. Vygotsky developed the concept of the "zone of proximal development" to highlight the significant relationship between teachers and learners. Applying the insights gained from observations, teachers bridge the gap between what children are capable of achieving independently and what they can accomplish through interactions with a more knowledgeable or skillful peer or adult.

Piaget also used observations extensively to discover how children construct knowledge. This learning takes place in stages through children's interactions with people and objects in their world. While Piaget's conceptual framework centers on invariant and universal progression through developmental stages, there are considerable individual differences in development and not every child fits neatly into these categories. Ritchie (2001) has questioned Piaget's premise of a single path of development and suggests that it causes adults to have rigid expectations of children's abilities.

Children's individual differences in learning and development are based on familial and cultural experiences that require adults to adapt their discipline strategies to meet their unique needs. While Vygotsky did not directly address the issue of the discipline of children, he also suggested that behavior was determined by social factors. Vygotsky and Piaget would concur that incorporating rules of behavior does not occur in a vacuum and requires a dynamic interplay between the child and the physical, social, and emotional environment.

Developmental discipline is based on the conviction that learning rules for behavior is a dynamic and constant process that begins in infancy and requires continued interaction and guidance from parents and teachers. The fluidity of an exchange between adult and child is dependent on the adult's willingness to look, see, and consider the many ways in which to respond.

Returning to the vignette featuring Darryl and Anthony, we see that the boys' conflict can be an important learning opportunity for them as well as for their teacher. Regular observations of Darryl and Anthony would provide their teacher with information about their temperament, their impulse control, their potential for aggression within the block area, and how they resolve their differences. When teachers take the time to actually document what they observe, they reflect, consider the many variables that contribute to behavior, and discover alternative responses. Learning how to effectively observe is discussed in detail in Chapter 3. Through ongoing observations of her students, Anthony's teacher might learn that Anthony does not generally hit other children. In these types of conflicts, Anthony's body language typically communicates warnings, and not threats.

Knowing that about Anthony, she might have waited and watched to see if the boys could work out their disagreement independently. Under the watchful eye of a teacher who will assist if necessary, children can learn the skill of conflict resolution. Sometimes, they can just work it out on their own without a teacher's interference. Encouraging children to solve their own problems conveys a sense of trust and confidence in their abilities and improves their future interactions. Most 5-year-olds are not yet able to fully articulate how they feel, nor are they consistently able to listen to other perspectives. Having opportunities to practice these skills, even very young children will develop the ability to problem solve. When teachers contribute to this learning process through modeling, offering suggestions, and providing words, they are demonstrating Vygotsky's (1978) zone of proximal development in action.

There still exists the possibility that Anthony could have hurt Darryl and that an active response by the teacher was necessary. Perhaps Anthony was taught at home to defend his property with aggressive or assertive behavior. However, if the teacher knew from past observations that hitting might occur in a situation such as this, she might not have allowed the children to be in the block area without close supervision. It is fairly common for children to argue when the space is limited, when the materials are in short supply, or when there is only one of the desired objects available. While classroom discord is inevitable, observation helps teachers prevent its escalation and the frequency of its occurrence. Through ongoing observations, teachers know those situations in their classrooms that are likely to be problematic and what is the best way to respond. Developmental discipline advocates different approaches based on each child's needs, his or her developmental level, and the presenting situation. It also encourages spontaneous and creative teacher responses when children's behavior is unpredictable.

THE DISTRACTED CHILD

Caitlin is a 7-year-old girl in first grade. Throughout the school year, Mrs. Baker has noticed that Caitlin is rarely on task and disrupts the class during structured lessons. She talks to her neighbors, rocks in her chair, and frequently asks to go to the bathroom. Caitlin repeatedly drops her pencil, then gets out of her seat to retrieve it. When this occurs, she will often poke her neighbor with the pencil. Mrs. Baker consistently corrects Caitlin's behavior verbally but is frustrated as the behavior persists.

Every teacher knows a child like Caitlin and can probably relate to Mrs. Baker's frustration. While Mrs. Baker's repeated attempts to reduce Caitlin's disruptive behavior were undoubtedly with the best of intentions, the outcome was not successful. The underlying reasons for Caitlin's behavior were not addressed.

Consider the many possible causes of Caitlin's inability to attend to Mrs. Baker's lessons. Perhaps Caitlin is not yet developmentally ready to participate in structured lessons during which she is asked to be still for an extended period of time. Some children innately have a higher activity level, which makes sitting and listening more challenging. It is also possible that Mrs. Baker has a limited tolerance for children such as Caitlin and that Caitlin's behavior is not really excessive. Mrs. Baker could perhaps be singling out Caitlin because of her misconceptions about Caitlin's ethnicity or prior knowledge of her family. Some teachers stigmatize children from particular ethnic groups and have low expectations for their behavior (Lubeck, 1994).

Learning issues may also play a role. Caitlin may be overwhelmed by the content of the lesson and misbehave as a means of getting attention or avoiding work that she is not able to master. Her distractibility and impulsivity could possibly be an indication of Attention Deficit Hyperactivity Disorder, (ADHD). Preoccupation with problems at home or interpersonal issues at school might also contribute to Caitlin's inability to pay attention. When the cause of the behavior problem is understood, interventions can be more finely tuned and are more likely to be effective.

Another important factor to consider is the fit between the child and the classroom learning environment. Every child comes to school with unique abilities, interests, and degree of willingness to learn. Learning is most effective and children be-

have best when teachers adapt their curriculum and teaching style to the needs of each child in the class. This approach is known as an emergent curriculum (Jones & Nimmo, 1994). In an emergent curriculum, children's interests, observations, and questions largely determine the content of what is taught. Motivation is considered a key factor in children's success in acquiring skills and knowledge. Engaging children through stimulating subject matter helps to channel their behavior in a constructive manner. Curriculum therefore emerges as a balance between children's choices, the teacher's values, the school's academic requirements, and the state's learning standards. Observation informs teachers about unique children's learning styles so that they can customize their teaching to best serve children. By learning more about Caitlin's issues through observation, Mrs. Baker's responses would be better aligned with her specific needs.

Developmentally appropriate practice, a framework for early childhood education (Bredekamp & Copple, 1997), also advocates that teachers be cognizant of children's developmental levels and build learning experiences around their abilities. However, children have unique timetables for growth and development, and therefore an individualized approach is necessary. Perceptions about children must be broadened to incorporate this diversity. Variations in behavior too must be understood within the context of these developmental levels as well as individual differences.

Developmental discipline takes into account who children are and how they learn within the context of their environment. At the same time, understanding ourselves as teachers with our own strengths and weaknesses is as important as understanding the child. Developmental discipline asks teachers to integrate their own temperaments, teaching styles, and past experiences with children. When teachers observe and reflect on their feelings and practice and separate their subjective experiences from what is actually seen, they become more adept at discipline. They may ask themselves:

- How did I respond to that child's behavior?
- Were my expectations realistic?
- What did I learn from the child and how can I modify my teaching and interactions for a better outcome in the future?

With developmental discipline, observations and reflections, coupled with an understanding of child development and culture, are central to predicting and preventing problem situations.

UNKIND BEHAVIOR

Mary, a third-grade teacher, is concerned that Michael is mean to Justin. Michael tells jokes about Justin to his classmates, taunts him during recess, and refuses to work with him on projects. Mary wants the children to get along well and intervenes whenever she sees Michael being unkind. She tells him to act nicely to his friends and to apologize for his actions. Michael complies with his teacher's requests but resumes his negative behavior when he believes she is not looking.

In addition to considering Michael's feelings, temperament, and experiences, the classroom environment must be examined in order to facilitate permanent change:

- Is it a community in which children and teachers learn to treat one another with respect?
- Are the rules and consequences clear, appropriate, and consistently reinforced?
- Is Michael learning the impact of his actions on his classmates?

Looking at Michael's behavior within the context of the classroom can be a window into planning effective interventions. Apparently, asking Michael repeatedly to behave nicely and to apologize is not working. Michael needs to learn that his behavior has repercussions not only for his victim but also for the entire classroom community. One possible intervention is to restrict Michael from working or playing with any of his peers when he exhibits hurtful behavior. Justin also needs to be supported in his efforts to stand up for himself and express his feelings. At the same time, Michael's other classmates can be encouraged to tell him how they feel about his unkind words and treatment of Justin. Regular class meetings during which feelings are shared, expectations are clarified, and rules are reinforced are vital to creating a successful classroom community (Charney, 2002). Class meetings are discussed in greater detail in Chapter 2.

To optimize Michael's positive behavior, his parents would need to be included in the process. They could share relevant information about Michael's relationships with children outside of school and problem solve with the educational staff about ways to help him. Furthermore, they would ideally reinforce strategies developed in school to provide consistency for Michael. Cultural differences between home and school may create obstacles, as this situation may be viewed with varying degrees of concern. With sensitivity and respect, educators and parents from diverse communities can come together to build a climate of mutual understanding (Springate & Stegelin, 1999).

It is important to keep in mind that all children act out. In fact, it is normal and healthy for children to assert themselves and test the adults in their lives. Recognizing that children must establish their autonomy as they grow, a process that at times manifests itself as defiance, promotes tolerance rather than anger and frustration about children's actions. However, inappropriate behavior cannot and should not be condoned. Through the use of developmental discipline, teachers can help children to respect and follow the rules while at the same time being cognizant of their underlying needs.

Developmental discipline is a conceptual framework, not merely a set of procedures. It is an approach that incorporates observations when rules, limits, and consequences are developed. These observations enable teachers to individualize responses to children. Research indicates that educators are most successful in classroom management when they use different strategies with different children (Marzano, 2003). Developmental discipline helps children regulate their own behavior and ultimately resolve conflicts. Teachers assist children in developing self-control without trying to control them. Children with self-control are more cooperative and competent members of not only their families and classrooms but also the larger community (Kaiser & Rasminsky, 1999).

FACTORS LEADING TO MISBEHAVIOR

Understanding the many factors that contribute to a child's misbehavior enables teachers to respond sensitively. In Figure 1.1 we present a list of factors that cause children to act out. Fatigue, illness, hunger, and poor nutrition affect children's overall development and most certainly their daily behavior. Inadequate housing, homelessness, and violence in the community undermine children's sense of security and may also contribute to difficulties in school. Family stressors such as divorce, illness, substance abuse, and even demanding work schedules may further influence children's feelings of self-worth and efficacy and subsequently their behavior. Peers too have a powerful influence on children's behavior in both positive and negative ways (Harris, 1998). Group contagion may also perpetuate misbehavior.

Individual temperaments may make it more difficult for some children to meet the demands of their environment (Thomas & Chess, 1996). Some children have an innate low tolerance for frustration, while others are impulsive. Oversensitivity to loud noises, crowds, or excessive visual stimuli is another characteristic that can compromise learning. A child who is experiencing speech and language delays, ADHD, or other learning or physical challenges may have a more difficult time following the rules of behavior in the classroom.

The classroom environment can sometimes deleteriously affect children's behavior. Too many children, cluttered and disorganized spaces, chaotic transitions, and overstimulation are just some of the factors creating stress in children. Developmentally appropriate practice advocates for limited class size and small teacher-child ratios (Bredekamp & Copple, 1997). Classrooms that do not adhere to these recommendations may result in increased conflicts among the children. Another dynamic within classrooms that can increase negative behavior are conflicts among the teaching staff. Differences in values, vision, teaching styles, expectations, and temperament are inevitable. Unless colleagues respect one another and engage in an active, ongoing dialogue to build their partnership, the children will sense any interpersonal tensions.

Ironically, teachers' excessive use of rewards and punishments can also negatively influence

Figure 1.1. Factors That Cause Children to Act Out

Emotional
- Temperament
- Anger
- Defiance
- Assertiveness
- Frustration
- Anxiety
- Fears
- Boredom
- Overstimulation
- Need for attention
- Jealousy
- Low self-esteem

Family
- Inadequate limit setting/excessive permissiveness
- Overly controlling discipline
- Sibling rivalry
- Demanding work schedule
- Work-related travel
- Relocation of home and school
- Divorce
- Substance Abuse
- Domestic violence and neglect

School
- Too many children
- Too much noise and stimulation
- Lack of developmentally appropriate curriculum
- Poor classroom organization (e.g., cluttered, too many toys)
- Competitive or violent games
- A "no" environment
- Lack of clearly stated and enforced rules

Physical
- Poor nutrition
- Hunger
- Fatigue
- Illness
- Pain
- Allergies

Learning Difficulties
- Developmental disabilities/delay
- ADHD
- Perceptual
- Auditory processing/Sensory integration
- Speech and language
- Pervasive Developmental Disorder
- Other special needs

Environmental
- Peer influence
- Seasonal factors
- Poor housing
- Poverty
- Violence in the community and in the media
- Terrorism and war

children's behavior (Kohn, 1999). While there is certainly justification for using behavior modification techniques in many situations, they only address the behavior at that moment and not the cause. When children are not simultaneously helped to cope with the underlying problem, behavior modification plans lose their effectiveness over time.

Through developmental discipline, educators teach children to follow the rules while respecting their emotional needs. Classroom management can be a positive experience for teachers and children when adults have the confidence and skills to clearly communicate their expectations to children. When teachers acknowledge children's feelings as well as their own while correcting behavior, children sense that they are respected and will comply more readily. Both societal forces and inner struggles may predispose children to be more vulnerable. Being compassionate in the face of these various obstacles and making the classroom environment supportive rather than overwhelming is an essential task for educators.

Teachers can use developmental discipline in conjunction with their work with families. Observations in schools are shared with parents to give them a clear picture of their child's functioning away from home. At the same time, parents are encouraged to communicate their experiences with their child at home as well as offer their own insights. This reciprocity between parents and teachers builds a bridge of consistency that results in happier and more self-controlled children.

THE UNPREPARED CHILD

Eight-year-old Jessica and her mother arrive at school 30 minutes late. Jessica has missed her school bus for the third time this week, and her mother is visibly angry because she is again late for work. With her hair unkempt, papers falling out of her backpack, and a pout on her face, Jessica enters the classroom. She has already missed her journal-writing time and cannot find the homework that she completed the previous night. When the teacher begins the math lesson, Jessica is feeling anxious about being able to do her work.

Jessica's school day is starting off poorly. Some children are able to bounce back from a chaotic morning and integrate themselves into the daily school routine. However, as is typical for many children, Jessica's late arrival and lack of preparedness have upset the beginning of her day.

Most educators would be worried about Jessica's repeated tardiness and its impact on her schoolwork. A concerned teacher might sit down with Jessica to find out what the problem is and convey her belief that Jessica is capable of doing much better. Another teacher could implement a reward system to encourage Jessica to submit her homework promptly. One may also choose to call home to discuss her lateness and brainstorm possible solutions. While these responses are all valid, there are additional ways of intervening.

Developmental discipline reminds us to look beyond a child's behavior and examine all possible reasons for that behavior so that teachers can respond most appropriately. It begins by asking some basic questions based on observations.

- Is this behavior ongoing or a new issue for Jessica?
- Is Jessica disorganized in her classwork or just in her homework?
- Is she keeping up academically?
- How does Jessica feel about the situation?

If this were a new problem for Jessica it might be beneficial to provide her with some strategies, such as packing her bag the night before, placing her homework in a special folder, and keeping a daily planner. In this case, helping Jessica to develop organizational skills would be more beneficial in the long run than just reprimanding her for not having her work done. Simply promising Jessica a reward might entice her to complete some assignments, but it is unlikely that she would acquire the skills to produce her work consistently.

It is also important to consider how Jessica's family manages routines:

- Is it only Jessica who has a hard time in the morning, or is the entire household in disarray?

- What time does Jessica go to sleep at night and what time does she awaken?
- Are the parents fully informed about the school's schedule and Jessica's assignments?

Clearly, language barriers and differing expectations of the child challenge parent-teacher communication. Yet collaborating is absolutely essential in customizing a positive solution.

When considering that Jessica herself is only one part of a larger family system, which contributes to her behavior, the possibilities for intervention become greater. Bronfenbrenner's (1979) ecological model suggests that issues affecting parents also affect children. A child's world is seen as a series of interrelated systems including the home, school, and larger community. Because of the interdependency of these various systems, educators must take them into account as part of their work with children. While our ultimate goal is to help children function well in and outside of school, children must be seen within the context of their family.

In communicating with families, teachers must be sensitive about the content of their message and its delivery. Simply informing Jessica's mother about the problem, something she is already aware of, could perhaps make her feel inadequate and resentful. She herself may be at her wit's end after making numerous attempts to help her daughter prepare for school. Parents often feel that teachers blame them for their child's difficulties, which can interfere with a positive working relationship. Jessica's mother might, as a result, be reluctant to share her concerns with the teacher for fear of being judged.

Communication between teachers and parents is a vital component of developmental discipline. Educators do not simply report to parents about problems but work with them on shared goals. Because children are part of both family and school systems, it is imperative that parental input is included and that efforts involve problem solving with the child and with the family as well. Broadening our lens to see the whole child and using that perspective to guide our behavior is the basis of developmental discipline.

SUMMARY

Throughout this chapter, vignettes have been used to illustrate behavior problems that teachers commonly face. Various strategies of developmental discipline were proposed as possible solutions. The following list summarizes the characteristics of the developmental discipline approach.

- It is a conceptual framework, not just isolated solutions to a problem
- It is an ongoing process from birth through adolescence
- It uses teachers' knowledge, insights, and expertise
- It encourages educators to observe children's individual temperaments, strengths, and weaknesses
- It allows teachers to understand and accept children for who they are and at their developmental level
- It helps teachers to integrate observations into their interventions
- It underscores the importance of reflective questioning
- It encourages teachers to examine their own teaching styles and relationships with children
- It promotes the adaptation of curriculum to meet the social, emotional, and cognitive needs of children
- It enhances communication in the classroom
- It minimizes conflicts and maximizes positive interactions
- It helps children to observe and understand their own behavior
- It teaches children self-control and accountability for their actions
- It empowers children to resolve their own conflicts
- It uses conflicts, spontaneity, and the unexpected as teachable moments for children
- It builds communication between teachers and parents working together on shared goals

The Relationship Between Discipline and Curriculum

Mrs. Reeves, a veteran teacher, has a traditional second-grade classroom. Children's desks are paired together, aligned in rows. Mrs. Reeves's desk is situated diagonally in the front left corner of the classroom. Bulletin boards are colorful and attractive, displaying children's work within various units of study. The room has three designated learning centers: the library, the computer, and math manipulatives. However, the materials in these centers are underused and do not reflect the ongoing learning. Mrs. Reeves, standing at the chalkboard, has just completed a lesson on three-digit addition with regrouping. She instructs the students to work on a series of problems independently at their seats. While most of the students are proceeding with the assignment, a few children are becoming restless and disruptive. Notes are being passed, paper airplanes are flying, and the noise level is gradually increasing. Mrs. Reeves reminds her students to get back to work.

Ms. Hanson's second-grade classroom is primed for hands-on, cooperative learning. Desks are arranged in clusters of four or five to facilitate group interaction. Ms. Hanson's desk is situated at the back of the classroom and is used primarily for student conferences. Center time is an integral part of the classroom routine in which children participate in learning activities independently and in small groups. A math lesson is currently under way, and Ms. Hanson is leading a group of five students while the rest of the class engages in a variety of problem-solving activities. The room is noisy and messy, and some children are moving about, not completing their work.

The teacher's pedagogy influences the classroom milieu, which in turn affects both the nature of learning and the behavior of the students. This milieu includes the physical layout, routines, learning activities, and social climate of the classroom. In both Mrs. Reeves's and Ms. Hanson's classrooms, we can see how learning and behavior are affected by the style of the teachers and how the lessons are structured. In other words, the children are responding not only to the content of the lesson but also to the manner in which the lesson is presented. While the majority of the children in both classes are following their teacher's assignment, others are not on task. Some children thrive in any educational setting because of their temperament and inherent abilities, while others require a more individualized approach. When teaching and learning styles do not match and the teacher is unaware of this mismatch, children are more likely to behave inappropriately. As the preceding vignettes illustrate, some children misbehave because the learning environment is not conducive to their temperament or individual needs or because expectations for behavior have not been clarified.

When exploring the different factors of why children act out, educators must look beyond behavior and be cognizant of children's unique social, emotional, physical, and cognitive needs to better adapt the curriculum. As pointed out in Chapter 1, teaching that incorporates a developmental discipline approach emphasizes observation as part of curriculum development and implementation. Yet there are other practical considerations that need to be acknowledged. Currently, state core curriculum standards (Carr & Harris, 2001) and high-stakes testing (Popham, 2001) drive public education. Educational initiatives, such as the federal No Child Left Behind Act (Executive Summary of the No Child Left Behind Act of 2001, 2001), seek to improve the academic performance of all children by mandating adherence to standards, maintaining consistency within and between schools, and making teachers accountable for students' achievement. As a result, teachers often lose control over the content of their lessons.

However, core curriculum standards articulate what is to be taught, not how to teach. Teachers continue to have choices in the manner in which they present their material. For example, in New York State, the English Language Arts Standard 1 states that students will read, write, listen, and speak for information and understanding (University of the State of New York, n.d.). One teacher might ask her students to read a biography, write a book report, and present it to the class. Another teacher might allow students to work in groups, research a topic of their choice, and write a play that dramatizes the essential themes. Creative application of curriculum as a means of engaging children can help diffuse as well as prevent misbehavior.

CURRICULUM DEFINED

What is the relationship between curriculum and discipline? How does curriculum influence behavior, and how does the behavior of the students affect the curriculum? When considering these questions, it is helpful to begin by defining *curriculum*. Simply stated, curriculum is a plan; a plan for teaching and for learning. It consists of many layers that address the who, what, where, when, why, and how of learning. Curriculum includes not only the specific areas of study but also the underlying values of a teacher, school, and community as well. These values form the foundation of the classroom, determine rules for behavior, and are related to all social interactions.

To better understand these implicit messages or values, we must look past the manifest content and structure of the curriculum. Teachers, when thinking about curriculum, may emphasize lesson plans and thematic units. These written curricula are essential for a well-run classroom and typically include goals and objectives, time frame, learning activities, and evaluation. Curricular plans may articulate the rationale for the particular area of study and the broader context in which the lesson takes place. Whether intending to or not, through lesson plans and thematic units, teachers convey their values about how children learn, what is necessary for them to learn, and how they are to behave in the classroom and beyond. These values are imbedded in and come from one's cultural history as well as educational background. The length of time spent on a topic and the level of enthusiasm can indicate how much the educator actually cares about that skill or concept.

Other values that are not necessarily considered a part of the curriculum but are nonetheless implicit in the teacher's plans are the rules for classroom behavior: listening, sitting quietly, cooperating, taking turns, and respecting the property of others. However, when these values are not made clear to the children, they lose their significance in the realm of classroom management. Regardless of the age of the learner, the importance of explaining and then reminding students of the rules and expectations for classroom behavior in a developmentally appropriate fashion cannot be underestimated. By making a conscious effort to emphasize the social guidelines for behavior, as a teacher would do with the specific subjects of a curriculum, teachers are able to actualize their belief systems.

One specific aspect of the curriculum in which teachers' values are inherently expressed is the physical environment. The design of the classroom space is inextricably linked not only to the learning but to the behavior of the students as well (Fields & Boesser, 2002). What materials are present in the classroom, where they are located, and the extent to which they are available to the students reflect the philosophy of the teacher, the school, or both. Early childhood educators typically invest a significant amount of time in designing their classrooms with elaborate learning centers (Stone, 2001). Montessori (e.g., 1965; 1967) and Olds (1987) both cite the physical setting as paramount in children's learning and well-being.

THE PHYSICAL ENVIRONMENT

The arrangement of desks, whether in clusters or in rows, influences the level of student interactions and the prevalence of group work. In Mrs. Reeves's classroom, the placement of desks encourages the students to focus primarily on the teacher, which supports her traditional, frontal teaching style. The desks in Ms. Hanson's class encourage peer interaction and small-group learning. This is not to suggest that group work is necessarily determined by the placement of desks. However, the configuration of the furniture, whether deliberately or randomly, conveys a message of how the group is to interact and also facilitates the primary means of learning in the classroom.

Children's behavior is affected by not only the placement of furniture and materials but also by the teacher's communication about the use of the classroom space. Whatever the setting and philosophy, children must be instructed and reminded of the expectations in that particular classroom. Mrs. Reeves and Ms. Hanson need to clarify when movement in the classroom and talking to peers are acceptable. The placement of desks in groups should not signal to the children that talking is always permissible. Rather, children need to be informed when group interaction is integral to the lesson and when they need to be quietly focused on the teacher or working independently.

Similarly, the presence of curricular materials in learning centers does not imply that they are available for use at all times. Understanding the parameters of center use is essential for children to maximize their learning potential. Before a lesson begins, at any grade level, the teacher must

establish clear guidelines on the use of classroom materials. For example, during frontal math lessons, Mrs. Reeves should encourage children to use manipulatives from the math center. However, the children are not permitted to obtain these materials at other times without permission.

When centers are being used, children need to know whether work is to be completed independently or with the assistance of peers or teacher. If children are having difficulty with a task, should they request assistance or do the best they can on their own? The teacher's role during center time is as vital as in whole-group lessons and must be thoughtfully planned and communicated to the children in advance. Additionally, rules regarding the maintenance of learning centers are critical to their success. Leaving the materials as they were found and cleaning up the workspace demonstrates a respect for property as well as for classmates who will use the center at a later time. Order in Ms. Hanson's class would be enhanced if she would regularly articulate the need for a neat classroom.

A teacher's methodology is translated not only through the physical environment but also in the manner in which learning takes place within that space. Learning can be an active or passive experience, and optimal classrooms strike a balance between the two. Both Mrs. Reeves and Ms. Hanson should expect students to sit quietly at their desks at times, while at other times engage in active exploration. Being in tune with their students' level of understanding will help them determine when a structured approach is needed and when students require hands-on experiences to develop a true understanding of concepts. Observing behavior during lessons informs teachers of who is on task and who needs additional assistance. Their willingness to be malleable and modify the original lesson plan in response to students' signals will contribute to a successful learning experience.

Frustration caused by a lack of understanding of the material can be a major cause of disruptive behavior in the classroom. Often, sitting for prolonged periods without an opportunity to move about can lead some children to misbehave. Some of the children in Mrs. Reeves's classroom might be restless because they have been at their desks too long. Perhaps they are struggling with the complexity of the subject matter or possibly are bored because they find the problems too easy. A frontal lesson to a whole group of heterogeneous students is not always the most effective way to teach. In any given class, children have different abilities and learning styles that must be identified and accommodated. While there are many advantages to a highly structured, teacher-directed curriculum as well as a more activity-driven, student-centered process, children can be lost in either program. When Mrs. Reeves and Ms. Hanson tune in to individual children within their classrooms, they learn about students' particular learning styles, timing and activity levels, ability to grasp new concepts, and struggles and strengths. Differentiation of instruction, meeting the needs of diverse learners within the same classroom, is rooted in observation and assessment (Tomlinson, 2001). Using teacher observations to "tweak" the curriculum is essential for students' achievement in any educational setting.

OBSERVATION

Teachers observe on many different levels. They use information gleaned from observations not only for curriculum development and implementation but also for preventing behavior problems. Teachers observe the interactions between students to determine under what circumstances intervention is needed. They learn over time which situations, social or academic, may precipitate a child getting into trouble. Group dynamics, which includes who is friendly with whom and who is on the periphery of the group, influence learning and the social composition of the class.

Comprehensive observations take into account overt behavior, verbalizations, dialogue, and non-verbal communication. Body language, gestures, and eye contact speak volumes about how children feel about themselves and their comfort level in the classroom environment. These indicators vary between cultures and may be misinterpreted or misunderstood as deviance or misbehavior. Equipped with rich data on the learning needs, behavioral issues, and cultural differences of individual children, teachers can revise the curriculum appropriately. For example, a teacher who notices that a child has difficulty cooperating within a particular group may choose to change the group composition or seating arrangement. A teacher may also decide to shorten or even stop a lesson based on observing the students. Observation gives teachers the tools to be flexible and to redirect the group. This redirection can take many forms, including a snack break, a stretch, engaging students in a discussion of the lesson, or perhaps introducing manipulatives or other hands-on activities to interrupt a negative interaction or further enhance understanding.

Teachers may also use observation as a means of self-reflection. Thoughtful introspection and reflective questioning based on observations of the children and oneself in the class leads teachers to fine-tune future interactions and curriculum. They can consider if their teaching style is effective in reaching every child and whether their tone and language are conducive to optimal learning. It is through observation that teachers can modify their own methodology as well as the curriculum to address both the learning needs and behavioral challenges of the children.

The students in Ms. Hanson's classroom are actively engaged in their studies, learning in small groups that match their skill level. However, behavior problems can arise in these types of settings when the teacher is not observing carefully or the expectations have not been clarified. Some students may see group work as an opportunity to get lost in the crowd or to defy their teacher. Other students may act out because they are having difficulty concentrating on their work in an overly stimulating environment. Still others may be doing their work, but are disruptive to the rest of the class because an appropriate noise and activity level has not been established.

It is in the gray area of curriculum, where expectations of the students are not clearly defined, that behavioral problems are more likely to occur. The developmental discipline approach, which advocates explicit guidelines, creates an environment in which children know what is expected of them. When uncertainty is minimized, children are more able to focus on the task presented to them. For students of all ages to function most effectively in school, they need rules and reminders about appropriate behavior to be presented in a structured and ongoing framework.

TRANSITIONS

Mr. Jordan has just completed a lengthy lesson on the colonial period and the American Revolution in his fifth-grade class. He has instructed his students to take their history textbooks to their lockers in the hallway and bring back their writing journals. If they have not already finished their writing assignment, they are to do so. Students who have completed their journal writing should wait at their desks until they are called by Mr. Jordan to conference with him. Some students exchange their books quickly and immediately begin to work, while others are considerably slower to return to their desks. As time goes on, more and more students are out of their seats, talking and disturbing those who are still writing in their journals. Mr. Jordan periodically reminds the students to return to their seats and to quietly wait their turn, but the noise level steadily increases.

One part of the school day that is typically challenging to both children and teachers, yet is often overlooked in the curriculum-design process, is transitions. Transitions are opportunities for teachers to clarify what is expected of children, yet these tend to be chaotic and to lack definition. They are those in-between times that are not necessarily planned for, such as lining up, cleaning up, moving from one lesson or activity to another, or waiting for dismissal. During these periods children often get into trouble because they typically do not know what they are to do and are not necessarily good "waiters." With mandated curricula becoming more demanding and the pressure for students to perform well on standardized achievement tests intensifying, teachers have an even greater need to maximize class time. Transitions must be seen as teachable moments and should not be wasted.

The transition between subjects can be stressful for both teachers and students, primarily because this time is not structured, as are other areas of the curriculum. Transitions may trigger a sense of uncertainty in children. Without definitive instructions during these "downtimes," a number of outcomes are possible. Children can get wild, perhaps out of control, because they lack a specific task. It is here that teasing, physical altercations, and even vandalism are likely to occur. Children may experience feelings of isolation or fear of being penalized because they are not conforming to the majority of the group. Some may feel anxious about who is in charge and what they should be doing at that moment. Children who are attempting to complete their work may be frustrated by the chaos around them. In Mr. Jordan's classroom, the lack of clarity during the transition period has created an excessively disruptive environment.

Clayton (1997) describes transitions as the "glue that holds the structure of the teaching day together" (p. 4). Whether children are moving from one location to another or from one subject to another, transitions set the tone for the activities that follow. Too frequently, precious learning time is wasted with lengthy and disorganized transitions. Teachers can facilitate quick, smooth transitions through meticulous planning and by either including children in that process or informing them of the rules. Observation by the teacher is crucial both prior to and during the transition period. When teachers thoughtfully consider the existing routines, the physical layout, and how students move within the classroom, they can "clean up" sloppy transitions.

If Mr. Jordan were to key into the behavior of the students in his class in between social studies and his next formal lesson, it would be apparent that many were not on task. At that point Mr. Jordan could evaluate why some of his students were not productive and consider how to modify the routine, the environment, and even his instructions. Mr. Jordan might recognize that the students needed to be supervised at their lockers because the temptation to fool around when a teacher is not watching is too great for many fifth graders. Since Mr. Jordan cannot hold his student conferences and be in the hallway simultaneously, one solution is to have students get their writing journals out of their lockers at the same time that they retrieve their history books. Fewer visits to lockers and cubbies mean less disruptions in the classroom.

One obvious problem in Mr. Jordan's classroom is that students have nothing to do once they complete their journal writing. In any class there are students who work more quickly than others. Teachers must anticipate this and provide students with a series or choice of activities to partake in during independent work periods to give children direction and a sense of purpose. Some possibilities are peer conferencing, silent reading, board or computer games, problem-solving tasks, brainstorming about an upcoming project, and even an opportunity to begin homework.

Mr. Jordan could further improve the dynamics in his classroom and transitions by clarifying and then enforcing a voice code. A voice, or noise, code is a system whereby the teacher explicitly communicates the expectations for noise or activity level at any given time. For example, a voice code of zero might signify no talking or moving about the classroom; one means whispers only, two is for soft conversations when students are working together, and three is for outdoor or gross-motor activities. In early childhood settings and in the lower elementary grades, voice codes may be accompanied by a visual representation such as a traffic light. Red could signify no talking, yellow means soft talking in the classroom, and green is for "outdoor voices." Voice codes are most effective when teachers use them consistently and give students ample opportunities to talk at appropriate times.

Waiting on line is another transitional time that is ubiquitous throughout the school day. Children are typically asked to stand on line to go to lunch, recess, specials, dismissal, assemblies, and even perhaps the bathroom. Without clear expectations for appropriate behavior, including talking and where to keep hands and feet, children are likely to get loud and invade one another's interpersonal space. Attention must be paid to the placement of children on line. It is not advantageous to have two children stand next to each other who either do not get along or typically act out when they are together. When necessary, teachers might alternate boys and girls on line or position themselves next to children who need additional supervision. Some students may need something to do while they are waiting. Singing songs or playing word or number games or even Simon Says are constructive ways to make time pass more quickly, thereby filling in the downtime. Children might be given a mental math problem to work on while they are waiting either inside or outside the classroom. For

example, a teacher in fifth grade might pose the following problems to solve while waiting: What is 596 plus 201? Or what is 16% of 25? A teacher could also ask children to think of the many ways to get to the number 24.

Preparation is essential for managing transitions effectively. Instituting warnings for an upcoming change not only alerts the children to what is coming but also demonstrates respect for their timing and work. It allows them to wind down and achieve a sense of closure and takes into account their need to make a cognitive shift. Any change in the external environment, including a variation of focus, activity level, or venue, requires children to make an internal adjustment. Teachers too must respond to changes that affect the children and curriculum. Depending on the style of the teacher and needs of the children, warnings may range from nonverbal signals such as dimming lights or playing a musical interlude to verbal reminders. Teachers might warn the children 5 minutes prior to the end of an activity or perhaps give them time cues throughout the work period. Through observation, teachers may note that certain children need a longer warning period or more reminders prior to the transition.

There are myriad ways that teachers can get children's attention in order to alert them about upcoming transitions or to redirect or reinforce behavior. Raising one's voice above the children's out of frustration or because it is part of one's style is a natural response. How else to get their attention? Some teachers may lower their voices to a whisper to engage the children. Others simply raise their hand, perhaps in a peace sign, to visually cue the children. Hand clapping to a pattern that requires students to listen and then imitate is also an effective strategy. Many teachers rely on rhyming verse such as, "One, two, three. All eyes on me."

Making the environment transition friendly is a necessary part of the curriculum. Creating sufficient pathways between desks and activity centers can alleviate congestion, which slows down transitions and precipitates altercations between children. Children's interpersonal space must also be considered important in environmental planning. Having fewer materials available at a given time may actually improve the classroom flow. Creative storage and rotation of learning materials will have a positive outcome in terms of children's behavior. Thoughtful placement of centers and materials, and frequent house cleaning, can minimize clutter, a way of life in many early childhood and elementary school classrooms. Veteran teachers assemble over the years a large collection of assorted resources. To make these collections most useful and not detrimental to the organization of the classroom, teachers must periodically review and then discard materials that are no longer relevant. Because teachers are likely to evolve in their teaching methods, so should the learning materials in the classroom. One formula to apply is to remove all papers, posters, books, boxes, games, toys, and items for recycling that have not been used in the past two years or that are broken or incomplete.

While classroom clutter can disrupt easy movement, insufficient materials that are poorly placed can also wreak havoc. For example, a teacher's asking children to come up to her desk to take a handout may lead to chaos if there is only one pile of handouts. Having more than one pile or assigning a few students to be responsible for handouts can expedite distribution. Some teachers choose to maintain an adequately stocked supply caddy at each table to save time and keep order. Marking storage areas and keeping them tidy will further improve classroom flow, as children know where things are.

CLASS AND COMMUNITY MEETINGS

One of the most effective ways to communicate expectations and facilitate smooth transitions is through group meetings. Class and community meetings are an integral part of developmental discipline. They are a time to share, explain, and reinforce rules of behavior and the inevitable consequences of breaking those rules. Meetings are a forum for students to develop their interpersonal skills, review past learning, reflect on behavior, and look forward to what is next. Children and teachers communicate concerns and ideas that facilitate positive group dynamics. Ideally, meetings should be scheduled on an ongoing basis to function preventatively or to address an immediate problem. Impromptu meetings are also beneficial for confronting issues that arise between regularly scheduled sessions. The best time to initiate this group format is at the beginning of the school year,

when patterns of behavior are being created, but teachers can introduce them at any time. The nature of these meetings is flexible, with the focus directed to the needs of individuals and the larger group. Meetings are actually an investment in time, ultimately creating more teaching and learning opportunities.

Charney (2002) talks extensively about class meetings in the "responsive classroom." She advocates creating an environment in which children feel comfortable saying what "they think and not what they think we want to hear" (p. 280). According to Charney, the primary goal of class meetings is to encourage open and honest communication. Additionally, she sees meetings as a way to help children learn to problem solve. DeVries and Van (1994) discuss the function of group time as that of being an opportunity for making rules, decisions, and discussing social and moral problems in the classroom.

Basic guidelines for class meetings must be established for them to be effective. Children can learn to communicate in a constructive, positive manner without blame, accusations, and labeling. Some children may be reluctant to share their feelings at meetings, particularly if they are at odds with the teacher or fear being penalized for their honesty. An anonymous suggestion or "feelings box" can address the concerns of children who are not comfortable expressing themselves verbally. Other children may use meeting time as an opportunity to provoke the teacher and seek attention for themselves. Teachers have a critical role in setting the tone for meetings. They plan the agenda, keep the group on task and on time, and also model and maintain a climate of respect, tolerance, and support. Teachers encourage children to listen to one another without interruption and to speak honestly to their peers. *Lashon hara*, Hebrew for "bad speech," is strongly discouraged because it involves talking unkindly about others, gossiping, and spreading rumors. Classes that hold meetings become environments where *lashon hara* is unacceptable, and children learn to talk directly to those with whom they have conflicts and to treat others with decency.

Charney (2002) suggests that classroom meetings take place at the same time every week. She believes that "meeting once a week gives children time to digest and reflect, and makes the procedure special" (p. 285). She proposes that meetings last

30–45 minutes, depending on the age of the children. Other educators (Bondy & Ketts, 2001; Kriete, 1999) recommend teachers hold morning meetings on a daily basis. They contend that daily meetings provide a sense of continuity and an opportunity to emphasis those critical values that foster community building: trust, respect, cooperation, and responsibility. Further, morning meetings are said to directly increase students' ability to attend, listen, and communicate. Early childhood educators have long understood the value of morning meetings and typically hold daily circle times to help transition children from home to school. Circle time usually includes discussion of the calendar, weather, plans for the day, and the sharing of stories and experiences. Morning meetings can go beyond circle time to incorporate more of the children's voices and ideas and at the same time clarify rules of behavior and expectations.

The developmental discipline approach includes classroom meetings as a central component of curriculum. Teachers needing to follow a mandated curriculum and meet established standards may be reluctant to devote precious class time to this medium. However, class meetings are possible in any setting and may even be as short as 15 minutes a week. To optimize limited class time, teachers can integrate content learning into their meetings by making associations between students' discussions and specific vocabulary, concepts, and current events.

Thoughtful planning of these meetings is essential. Such planning includes observations of the individual students and the group, timing, location, and seating arrangement. Consideration must also be paid to how long students are allowed to speak so that they learn to share and not interrupt or monopolize the discussion. One strategy is using an egg timer to clearly delineate the time for each speaker and to keep the meeting moving along. Eventually, students develop the ability to express themselves more succinctly. Teachers should also determine ahead of time if students will sit on the floor in a circle or at their desks and whether every student has to be positioned in the same way.

In accordance with the individualized approach of developmental discipline, teachers may need to experiment and observe the results to determine the best time, space, and procedure for their meetings. It can sometimes be challenging to elicit student's expression of feelings. Games and activities are effective techniques for facilitating communication. For example, a teacher may ask two children who have had a conflict to role-play by switching identities with one another. Teachers may also present hypothetical situations for the students to ponder. Students may be asked, "What would you do if your friend asked to copy your homework?" or "What would you do if you found a wallet with $100 in it?" Teachers may also focus their meetings on a theme or concept such as friendship, trust, respect, or courage. Social skills programs, such as the Open Circle (Seigle, Lange, & Macklem, 2003), provide educators with a structure for guided class meetings. These curricula are most valuable with novice teachers because they provide a script and minimize planning time. As with any curriculum, teacher training helps to ensure that the faculty is knowledgeable about the program, supported throughout the initial process, and better able to implement it successfully.

The community meeting, a variation of the class meeting for third grade and up, consists of a larger group of students coming together to share ideas and concerns. Similar to what occurs in the more intimate class meeting, rules and expectations are emphasized. Community meetings may consist of an entire grade level or a wing of the school with mixed age groups.

Because the group is significantly larger, an organized procedure is essential for the group to be most productive. It is recommended that items for discussion be identified ahead of time and student representatives be chosen to facilitate the group process. Student representatives, or speakers, should be rotated to provide students who wish to participate with that opportunity. This may be accomplished through elections or a random drawing of names. As in classroom meetings, topics can be generated from both student and faculty observations and experiences. The frequency and duration of these forums must again be in accordance with the scheduling logistics of the particular school, but every 4–6 weeks is a reasonable guideline.

Community meetings serve as a form of checks and balances for the larger school system in terms of the way teachers, administrators, and students talk to one another. It is imperative for all school personnel, from the principal to the lunchroom monitor, to model respect, kindness, and good manners. Whether the interactions take place in formal meetings or informal settings, such as hallways, lunchrooms, and faculty lounges, members of the community need to be sensitive to the content and tone of their language.

A possible focus within community meetings is the planning of community-service projects. It is a powerful experience for children to be part of the decision-making process and to participate in a group charity or volunteer effort. Students can advocate for a particular institution or activity by researching the organization and then presenting that research to the group. For example, some students might want to serve food in a soup kitchen, contribute to a clothing drive, or institute a letter-writing campaign. Individual classes or groups of students can follow through by taking responsibility for specific tasks related to the community project.

CONTRACTS

Contracts are a natural extension of classroom or community meetings. They are an effective means with which to concretize the goals of both the teacher and students and can help facilitate follow-through. Contracts may address a specific academic or behavioral problem or the general rules within the classroom or school. An evaluation process needs to be implemented to ensure that the contract has been adhered to.

One can imagine how classroom meetings and subsequent contracts might improve the overall environment in Mrs. Reeves's, Ms. Hanson's, or Mr. Jordan's classes. The teachers could address the disruptive behavior of the students and brainstorm with them possible causes and realistic solutions. When students are engaged in the contract-writing process, they assume a sense of ownership and commitment to the agreed-upon goals. See Figure 2.1 for an example of a classroom contract.

A community contract may also be indicated when rules are formulated for the entire school, such as in the use of computers. All students must sign and adhere to the contract, which may include not accessing inappropriate Web sites or students creating their own Web sites.

Additionally, contracts can be used on a more individualized basis to address a student's social,

Figure 2.1. Class Contract

We, the students of class 4-H, developed a list of rules for our classroom on September 5, 2002. It is important to have rules to guide our behavior while living, learning, and working in a school community. This contract reminds us of what is appropriate and expected of us. The following is our list:

- Respect yourself and others; speak kindly to and about other people.
- When someone is speaking, listen, show him or her courtesy, and pay attention.
- Raise your hand when you want to say something.
- Listen to directions, follow instructions, and work quietly.
- Clean up your mess, and help clean up the mess of others.
- Respect property.
- Keep yourself and others safe.

We have agreed that these are the guidelines we will follow. The members of this class have promised to follow these rules to make our school life the best it can be.

_____
[Teacher's signature]

_____
[Learning specialist's signature]

_____
_____
_____
_____
[Students' signatures]
_____

behavioral, or academic issues. Rather than calling excessive attention to a child who is acting out during a lesson, the teacher may work with the child to create a personal contract. When behavior is carefully documented through ongoing observations, teachers can monitor how the child is doing and adjust the contract accordingly. Did both parties keep their ends of the bargain? Were any consequences enforced as dictated by the contract? All contracts need to be reviewed on a daily basis and modified as needed. Modifications may include adding a behavioral goal or raising the expectation regarding a particular behavior. Ideally, a contract is used for a limited period of time, with the hope that the improved behavior is internalized.

> Sarah, a third grader, regularly calls out to her teacher, Mrs. Taylor, without raising her hand. Mrs. Taylor recognizes that her frequent reminders for Sarah to behave appropriately seem to be reinforcing Sarah's disruptive behavior. She decides to meet with Sarah to discuss Sarah's difficulties and include her in the problem-solving process.

In preparation for her meeting with Sarah, Mrs. Taylor reflects on Sarah's disruptiveness in conjunction with the overall classroom environment. She reviews how rules for classroom behavior have been communicated. Mrs. Taylor notes that while most students continue to raise their hands to get her attention, Sarah's calling out has had a contagious effect on some students. She remembers that when Sarah is absent students consistently raise their hands to be called on. Perhaps the students see that calling out gets the teacher's attention more quickly than raising hands. Sometimes merely responding to negative behavior reinforces it. It is very easy for teachers to fall into the trap of answering students who enthusiastically call out. Resisting the urge to reply to interested students is necessary to send a clear message about classroom rules.

Mrs. Taylor hopes to further help Sarah modify her behavior by developing a contract between them to remind Sarah of the expectations regarding classroom participation. Although Mrs. Taylor has a specific agenda for her meeting with Sarah, she still wants to include Sarah. After all, if Sarah actively participates in problem solving she will be more invested in the solution.

In the course of the meeting, Mrs. Taylor reemphasizes the need to follow the rules for communication and listens to Sarah's explanation for her behavior. Sarah articulates that she feels that the smart kids are always called on first and she is frustrated when not recognized. Mrs. Taylor hears this response and proposes to Sarah that they make a deal in the form of a contract. In the contract, Sarah agrees to raise her hand, and Mrs. Taylor will make an extra effort to call on Sarah first (see Figure 2.2). Mrs. Taylor understands that habits are

Figure 2.2. Example of a Student-Teacher Contract

First-Week Contract Between Sarah and Mrs. Taylor

Date_____

Sarah's Goals

- I will raise my hand at least five times a day and wait to be called on by Mrs. Taylor.
- I will remain in my seat while raising my hand.
- I will remain quiet while my hand is raised.

Mrs. Taylor's Goals

- I will make every effort to call on Sarah first when she raises her hand.

When we meet these goals, a second contract will be written.

_____

[Sarah's signature]

_____

[Mrs. Taylor's signature]

hard to break, so for the first week Sarah would be expected to raise her hand only five times throughout the day and Mrs. Taylor would call on her immediately. The contract would be revised when Sarah has mastered this first step. The goal is for Sarah to increase her hand raising with the understanding that she would not be called on first every time. When this second goal has been met, the subsequent contract would stipulate that Sarah would always raise her hand and that Mrs. Taylor may or may not call on her.

Certain children may initially need additional reinforcement to meet their goals. Mrs. Taylor believed that Sarah being recognized in a timely fashion was reinforcement enough. Under certain circumstances, external rewards may be indicated. For example, a teacher could allow a child to read a book to the class, write on the chalkboard, or help decorate a bulletin board as an incentive. However, when a teacher's first response is to use external rewards such as stickers and promises of pizza parties, children's natural inclination to behave appropriately is lessened (Kohn, 1999).

While contracts may be a powerful tool for fostering behavioral changes, they often lose their effectiveness when the novelty wears off. Sometimes the need for contracts diminishes when the child has accomplished the stated goals. In other circumstances, the contract may be rewritten to better motivate the child. Close supervision of the process and the dynamics between student and teacher is necessary to determine the duration of the contract. There are times when a contract is no longer useful, and another strategy must be introduced.

When a contract is developed between teachers and students, parents are generally informed of the nature of the problem and ensuing intervention. Including parents in this process will further reinforce the child's following through on the contract. Parents may even be included in the planning of the contract and sign it along with the student and teacher. For example, when the issue is completing homework or getting to school on time, parents are an important variable.

HOME–SCHOOL CONNECTIONS

Sometimes parents ask teachers and administrators for assistance with behavior management at home. They may be experiencing similar conflicts and need help in handling the situation at home. Educators can suggest to parents that they use the same strategies of developmental discipline. These include clarifying expectations and observing to determine logical consequences. Family meetings, a variation of classroom and community meetings, can encourage dialogue about feelings, ideas, and concerns and facilitate group problem solving. Contracts are also an effective way to follow through with agreements made at family meetings.

CONCLUSION

Meetings, contracts, observation, and thoughtful planning are various tools that enhance curriculum implementation. When teachers see behavior and learning as interdependent, a dynamic relationship ensues. Curriculum and behavior must complement each other for the instruction to be effective, resulting in the acquisition of concepts, knowledge, and skills. Recognizing children's needs and tailoring lessons to them may circumvent many disciplinary problems. Educators constantly make choices about how they teach and respond to children. The developmental discipline approach empowers teachers to customize their teaching to respect and accommodate the children within the learning process. Specifically, building on this chapter, we recommend that teachers do the following:

- Observe children as they engage in learning tasks
- Adapt the curriculum and teaching style to the individual learner
- Change the classroom setup, activity, and location and pace of the lesson to maintain students' focus
- Plan for transition and downtime
- Convey clear expectations for students' behavior
- Conduct classroom and community meetings

CHAPTER 3

Building Observational Skills

Mrs. Korn has been teaching third grade for more than 25 years and considers herself adept at meeting her students' needs. However, this year, she has a student who is particularly troubling and Mrs. Korn does not know how to help her. Samantha rarely smiles or laughs, never raises her hand, and is reluctant to participate in discussions or group activities. She does not seem to have any friends in the class. The other students report that Samantha lies and is not nice. Mrs. Korn finds Samantha to be extremely whiny, clingy, and manipulative. Samantha repeatedly asks to go to the nurse with various physical complaints, which affects her class work. The high quality of Samantha's homework is not necessarily indicative of her capabilities, as Mrs. Korn suspects Samantha may not be doing her own work at home. When Mrs. Korn consulted with Samantha's second-grade teacher, she was told that Samantha did struggle a bit academically and was relatively quiet in class but had no major problems.

How can Mrs. Korn better understand Samantha's difficulties so that she can intervene effectively? Stepping back and formally observing as well as gathering pertinent information from those involved in Samantha's life will help Mrs. Korn see Samantha more clearly. What does Mrs. Korn need to know in order to address her concerns about Samantha's social, emotional, behavioral, and academic functioning? One direction for inquiry might be Samantha's social interactions: her relationships with peers, teachers, parents, and possibly siblings. A closer look at Samantha's ability to connect with others and sustain meaningful relationships will help Mrs. Korn assess the situation. Mrs. Korn will need to observe how Samantha communicates feelings and if her affect is appropriate. Samantha's behavior in school and her level of academic achievement also need to be documented to gain a more complete picture of her overall development. These inquiries contribute to a comprehensive observational program.

As we pointed out earlier, observation is an integral part of evaluation and intervention. It enables teachers to assess a child's specific strengths and weaknesses and then effectively facilitate growth and change. Thoughtful, systematic observation can alert educators to subtle problems that might otherwise be overlooked. However, too often, the formal observation process is reserved for children having significant difficulties and omitted from routine work with children.

Regular observations are useful because they are a starting point for conversations between colleagues in an effort to help children. Having multiple perspectives can also help to minimize observer bias. When teachers communicate observations of children to administrators, other educators, therapists, and parents, children's needs are more likely to be met. An effective team discusses the observations, brainstorms, and suggests the most appropriate methods of intervention. This pertains to typical school-related challenges such as completion of homework, keeping up with demanding class work and peer struggles as well as more serious issues including developmental delays, language difficulties, and learning differences.

As discussed in Chapter 2, observation is also a central component in curriculum development. When teachers plan their lessons and activities, they need to consider the various levels of skills and comprehension within their classroom. Recorded observations of children at work and at play provide teachers with knowledge of their academic level, learning styles, and interests. The most successful teachers will modify their plans to address students who need additional support and those who are quick learners and need extensions or enrichment. For example, Mrs. Korn could use her observations in her teaching by assigning Samantha to work groups that are particularly cooperative or by providing oral directions if Samantha has had difficulty deciphering written instructions.

Classroom management can also be improved with the integration of an ongoing observation process. Typically, teachers do not formally plan for disciplining children or the prevention of discipline problems. When they do, the plan tends to be a rigid formula that sets the rewards and consequences ahead of time and does not take into account the individual child. Incorporating an observational system enables teachers to develop strategies that fit the specific behavioral patterns of children within their classroom. If Mrs. Korn were to document Samantha's positive and negative interactions, she would be more aware of the unique situations or dynamics of children that might elicit Samantha's behavioral difficulties. For example, Mrs. Korn might note that Samantha's lying only seems to occur when she is with a particular group of children. This piece of information might lead Mrs. Korn to wonder if Samantha feels inadequate with those children and if her need to fit in would compel her to lie. Mrs. Korn could then make a special effort to be around when Samantha is with this group and help her to contribute more constructively.

Another use of observations is in teacher-parent communication. Teachers can share observations, relating not only to academic performance but also to social and emotional development. Parents may be more receptive to a teacher's views when they are substantiated with objective observations.

Whether a teacher is reviewing positive aspects of a child or discussing concerns, observations can make parent-teacher conferences and informal communications more meaningful. Likewise, parents who observe systematically to get a better handle on their children could present pertinent information to teachers. For example, if Samantha's parents were to keep track of her behavior while she was doing homework and then share those details, Mrs. Korn would have a more in-depth view of Samantha's work habits and academic abilities. Samantha's parents could also carefully note her interactions with friends in the neighborhood, making it clear whether Samantha's difficulty socializing with peers was restricted to school or also manifested itself in other settings. Additionally, Samantha's parents would be vital in reporting about Samantha's affect outside of school and the existence of any physical ailments. Including parents in the observation process by having them actually record and then communicate their findings extends the benefits of developmental discipline by incorporating parent expertise.

THE OBSERVATION PROCESS

There are several distinct steps in the observation process: planning, objective observation/documentation, interpretation, assessment/recommendations, and intervention/follow-up. These steps are cumulative and cyclical. The observational regimen can be carried out within a finite period of time or can be ongoing to address long-term difficulties or concerns. Ideally, all relevant adults in a child's life would be included and would meet periodically as a team to review the progress.

Step 1: Planning

The first step in the observation process is planning. Here the teacher considers the purpose of the observations and what is to be accomplished. Reflecting on an existing problem and all the contributing variables enables one to set goals to keep the observations focused on relevant behavior. Planning includes deciding the location of, timing of, duration of, and even whom to include in the observations. A clarification of responsibilities can ease any later confusion about roles. A method for recording behavior is also selected; more than one may be desirable. The choice of observational recording techniques depends upon the nature and frequency of the behavior problem, the contexts in which the behavior is manifested, and the personal preferences and comfort level of the observers. (Recording methods will be discussed in greater detail in a later section of this chapter.) Anticipating potential obstacles such as limited time and resistance by colleagues or parents is also an essential part of the planning. While modifications in the process are inevitable, as a result of the information that is gathered, planning for observations provides direction and focus.

Goal setting begins by highlighting what is already known about the child. With Samantha, it has been noted that she rarely smiles or laughs in school, seeks attention from her teacher in negative ways, fabricates, does not actively participate in class, does not interact appropriately with peers, and frequently reports that she does not feel well. Additionally, what Mrs. Korn does not know about Samantha will contribute to future inquires. For example, Mrs. Korn does not know if Samantha exhibits similar behaviors outside her class. Mrs. Korn's goals for the observational process will therefore include formal observations of Samantha in a variety of activities, including transitions, lunch, recess, specials, arrival, and dismissal. Observational planning does not take place in isolation. In order to optimize this process, Mrs. Korn will work collaboratively with her colleagues to ensure a thorough examination.

Step 2: Objective Observation/ Documentation

The heart of this process, the recording of objective observations, can be particularly difficult. One must gather authentic, pertinent information without tainting that data with personal opinions or judgments. Eliminating all subjectivity is not realistic. However, a reasonable expectation is to minimize as much bias as possible. This is accomplished in part by reflecting on one's own unique perspectives, philosophies, lifestyle, and culture. A good observer acknowledges how past experiences as a teacher and as a member of a family or specific ethnic or socioeconomic group might influence perceptions and attitudes.

Examining how culture illuminates our field of vision is critical (Lynch, 2000). Culture shapes not only our behavior but also our attitudes about how others behave. While it is important to respect ethnic, racial, and religious differences, understanding others' viewpoints and behaviors can be difficult when identification with a culture of origin is strong. For example, a teacher may interpret a child's aversion of eye contact as suspicious. However, in the Asian community direct eye contact is considered a sign of hostility and disrespect, and children are taught not to look directly at others (Chan, 2000). This is also true in Native American communities, where children are encouraged to refrain from using direct eye contact (Joe & Malach, 2000). Knowledge of the values of various cultures of children in classrooms enhances teachers' ability to relate appropriately and observe more objectively. A teacher's own upbringing may influence her views about how children should be dressed for school and how they are to speak to adults. However, these expectations might not fit with what is acceptable or typical in that particular population. Leaping to conclusions based on a narrow vision will affect the integrity of the observations.

Even videotapes can fall victim to the observer's bias. When the videotape is turned on and off, the width of the visual field and the direction of the video camera are chosen by the viewer and therefore contribute to the outcome. The Hawthorne effect (Feldman, 2002), which suggests that the act of observation itself changes the nature of what is being seen, is always operational. Many factors can affect observations. These may include mood, the environmental conditions in which the observation takes place (e.g., temperature, lighting, seating), fatigue level, familiarity with the child being observed, feelings for the child, and the enthusiasm of the observer. Whether the observer is engaged or participating in the interaction or watching from afar is yet another component to consider when interpreting an observation. Having the luxury of observing without direct responsibility for the children provides an added degree of perspective. Additionally, the skill level of the observer will most certainly affect the quality of the observations.

How do educators record with a minimal intrusion of bias? Being cognizant of its inevitable presence is as essential as recognizing the individual's role within the observation dynamic. Despite the anticipated presence of one's own bias, springing from the issues noted here, a proficient observer is trained to distinguish what is actually seen or heard from what is presumed to be occurring. Separating objective observation and subjective inference is key to minimizing bias. For example, if Mrs. Korn were to observe Samantha sitting with a group of peers during lunchtime and conclude, as a result, that she was making friends, her perceptions could be inaccurate. Samantha's merely sitting adjacent to classmates does not necessarily indicate that she is engaging in relationship building. It is possible that she was there for lack of another seat. Observers must be cautious not to readily infer, but rather to carefully consider, all the possible motives for behavior. Even then, inferences must be understood for what they are: conclusions logically drawn from evidence. Inferences are not facts. Similarly, Mrs. Korn could erroneously assume from Samantha's reticence in class that she is not prepared, when in actuality Samantha is too shy to participate.

One way to learn to distinguish between description and interpretation of behavior is to literally draw a dividing line down the center of a paper. What is actually observed is separated from opinions, judgments, and feelings about what is seen. (See Appendix A for a sample Observation Training Form, which is based upon an observation model developed by A. Axtmann and Leo Pascua and used at the Rita Gold Center at Teachers College, Columbia University.) Using this form within a variety of settings, keeping the focus on the child, and then sharing those observations with colleagues to obtain feedback, will help to sharpen one's recording skills. It does take time to effortlessly clarify the differences between objective observation and inference, but once that skill is honed bias will be significantly decreased. We suggest that over time, using the Observation Training Form and sharing the results will help to minimize bias in future observations. Figure 3.1 shows how Mrs. Korn might complete the Observation Training Form while observing Samantha in her classroom.

Step 3: Interpretation

When enough information has been gathered from a variety of sources, the behavior can then be interpreted to determine its meaning. As previously suggested, arriving at this step prematurely may yield an inaccurate understanding of the situation. Given Mrs. Korn's past observations of Samantha's difficulties with peers, it would not be surprising if she automatically blamed Samantha for her inability to work productively in her rain forest group. However, keeping an open mind might lead Mrs. Korn to acknowledge that other factors may be operative. Mrs. Korn's observation of Samantha in this group raises questions not only about Samantha's social skills but also about how her peers relate to her. No one in Samantha's group responds to her question about the tasks, and the children appear to exclude and even antagonize her during the decision-making process. It is possible that this dynamic is pervasive in her classroom experiences. This social-emotional climate may have significant implications for Samantha's behavior, in that she may feel both isolated and rejected. That may explain some of her attention-seeking behavior, her sad affect, and even her need to find solace from Mrs. Korn or the school nurse. However, the behavior of her peers does not exonerate Samantha's own responsibility to behave appropriately. Clearly, these issues must be addressed from both an individual and a group level.

When Mrs. Korn sits back and puts this observation in context with her initial concerns, questions about Samantha's cognitive abilities are also inevitable. Samantha seems to have trouble paying attention, is a poor listener, and does not offer anything constructive to group efforts. What is not known is whether Samantha's frustrations with her peers have contributed to her low academic achievement or if inherent cognitive difficulties have been the basis for her weak group-learning skills. Perhaps both factors may be relevant here. In either case, there is a need to further explore Samantha's ability to learn in different contexts: independently, one-on-one with an adult, and in different peer groups.

Step 4: Assessment/ Recommendations

Looking at the data from multiple perspectives provides a comprehensive assessment and finely tuned recommendations. In Samantha's case, incorporating her parents in the process was critical in illuminating the possible causes of her struggles in the classroom. In the team meeting, which

Figure 3.1. Observation Training Form

Observer <u>Mrs. Korn</u>   **Date** <u>December 4, 2001</u>

Directions

- Record child's name and age.
- Record observer's name and date.
- Describe the context
  - a) physical setting
  - b) situation

- Note the time at regular intervals (include beginning and ending time).
- Record exactly what the child does in the behavioral descriptions column.
- Record your interpretations/inferences.

- -

Child's Name <u>Samantha</u>   **Child's Age** <u>8</u>

Context:

Physical Setting: Third-grade classroom. Students' desks arranged in groups of four. My desk is in the front, left-hand corner facing the door. The room contains learning centers and cubbies as well as bulletin boards with students' completed work.

Situation: I have just given the class a set of instructions for the rain forest project. The children are to work in groups of four focusing on one particular rain forest animal. Samantha's group has been assigned the Howler monkey. There are 24 students in the class at this time.

Time	Behavioral Descriptions (objective)	Interpretations/Inferences (subjective)
9:40 a.m.	Samantha sits with her group, looking through her rain forest folder, while the other three students discuss how to assign the tasks.	
	Samantha asks what the different tasks are as Joe is speaking. Samantha is told by Joe that she is to report on what the Howler monkey eats.	Samantha was not paying attention. No one answers Samantha's question directly. She was not part of the decision-making process.
9:41	Samantha states loudly that she does not want that task. She wants to report on where the Howler monkey lives. Samantha is told that that task was assigned to Robert.	Samantha's tone is whiny and demanding. The group is not working effectively.
9:41	Samantha states that I said she could research where Howler monkeys live. Samantha stares at the cubbies while Robert says, "No way. That's my job."	I had not said that to Samantha.
9:42	Samantha raises her voice and says, "You have to give me that job. I had it first."	Samantha seeks attention by being oppositional. She is unwilling or unable to compromise.
9:42	She gets up from her seat and walks to me while I am working with another group. Samantha interrupts me, crying, and says that her group is not being fair to her.	Samantha interrupts for the second time.
		She has a low threshold for frustration and poor impulse control. Also, poor problem-solving and conflict-resolution skills. The students in Samantha's group were not receptive or kind to her.

included Samantha's parents, Mrs. Korn, the school nurse, and the school psychologist, it was revealed that, during the recent adoption of twin infants into the family, Samantha had learned she also was adopted. Some of Samantha's social awkwardness may be in response to these major changes within the family, considering that Samantha did not have any significant trouble with peers in the previous school year. The school psychologist might suggest

individual play therapy or a social skills group to explore Samantha's observed sadness and to better understand her difficulties within the classroom.

Questions regarding Samantha's cognitive abilities were raised by observations of performance within the classroom as well as by the discrepancies between her home and schoolwork. Samantha's parents acknowledge that struggle and resistance characterize homework time, and they often complete the work for her. Her low frustration tolerance, impulsivity, and limited attention span, which is seen at home as well as at school, raise questions about her learning abilities. A thorough evaluation through a private educational psychologist or the district's child study team would indicate the presence of a learning disability. Given Samantha's chronic physical complaints, which warrant numerous trips to the nurse, this evaluation should include a complete medical and a possible neurological exam to rule out any pathology. The findings could have a profound impact on Samantha's learning and behavior.

It is important to gauge Samantha's parents' response to her problems before making recommendations such as therapy, an educational evaluation, or even a medical exam. The parents' acceptance and willingness to move forward on these recommendations may take time. Families with little prior experience navigating through bureaucracy may resist the intervention. During initial meetings with parents, team members may just want to plant a seed or help prioritize which step to take first. Educators need to be patient with parents and understand the different factors that might contribute to their reluctance.

At the same time, Mrs. Korn could help Samantha by modifying her work both at school and at home. The purpose of these modifications would be to create successful academic experiences, thereby building on her self-esteem. Mrs. Korn might consider pairing Samantha with children who have been friendly to her this school year as she recognizes that some children have not been particularly kind or cooperative with Samantha. According to her parents, Samantha has shown no difficulties with peers outside school and has many friends from after-school activities and the neighborhood. It is possible that Samantha's social difficulties at school may be a result of not only the group dynamics but also her learning issues. Mrs. Korn might consider instituting classroom meetings focusing on promoting positive communication, conflict resolution, and building an environment of mutual support and acceptance.

Step 5: Intervention/Follow-Through

Intervention is the final phase in the observational process, when recommendations are carried out on the basis of interpretation of the collected data and the overall assessment of the particular child and situation. This includes a follow-through agreement attesting that all team members are aware of their responsibilities and ensuring that suggestions are implemented. For example, the school psychologist might follow up with the parents by telephone to see if they have any additional questions or if they need help in finding the necessary resources. Ideally, the psychologist might observe periodically in Mrs. Korn's classroom to determine if there have been any improvements with Samantha, her relationships with her peers, or the overall classroom tone. Regular team meetings would be held to review Samantha's progress and reassess her goals.

The Challenges of the Observation Process

The overall observation process in a real-life school setting may present a major challenge. Teachers report that there is little or no time for observation given the rigorousness of the curriculum and the special activities that children attend. Often, teachers are on their own in the classroom, which makes observation a logistical obstacle. They assert that they already feel overwhelmed with their workload and cannot take on another responsibility. Clearly, the administration must stress the importance of observation for it to be incorporated into the daily pedagogical routine. Ongoing support and training in the various observational methods, skills, and techniques is also recommended. Every teacher needs to develop her own system for documentation. Using clipboards, index cards, or a tape recorder are ways to facilitate the process.

Creating observational opportunities within the classroom can be particularly daunting, both spatially and temporally. Choosing to be a participating observer or recording behavior from the periphery present unique problems that can be overcome with practice. Blending into the woodwork is no easy feat for a teacher who is accustomed to interacting with and responding to the children at all times. At the same time, recording observations while being solely responsible for the entire class takes organization, finesse, and patience. Within the constraints of being a solo practitioner, it is imperative to upgrade one's teaching through observation.

OBSERVATIONAL METHODS

The narrative observation, as illustrated in the Observation Training Form (Appendix A) is not the only means of recording, and several other observation methods will be presented in this section.

Narratives

Narratives or narrative observation is a preferred method because of the rich data it yields. Also known as *running records* or *specimen descriptions* (Bentzen, 2001), narratives document a continuous stream of behavior and its naturally occurring context. No preparation is necessary and observers have flexibility in terms of length, location, type of behavior, and the number of children included in the observation. The narrative, which can also be in paragraph form with interpretations at the end, ideally includes a context description consisting of two sections: the physical setting and the interpersonal situation (Bentzen, 2001). A detailed narrative of just 1 to 3 minutes can highlight a substantial amount of meaningful behavior. Of course, behavior patterns can only be discerned when children are observed over a period of time in various situations. Narratives may be difficult for the unskilled observer and take considerable practice. Appendix B contains an alternative narrative report, which provides structure and guiding questions. Observers consider these questions when focusing on salient behaviors. The questions do not necessarily require answers but are useful when organizing, evaluating, and summarizing the data in the Narrative Observation Report. Some of the questions are not relevant to infant, toddler, and preschool-aged children and therefore should simply be omitted.

Checklists

Checklists are another observation method commonly used by teachers because they are quick and user friendly. The observer simply notes the presence or absence of specified behavior. Teachers often use checklists to measure the acquisition of skills and concepts and to examine behavior. See Appendix C for an example of a checklist assessing peer interactions. Figure 3.2 is an example of the checklist using Samantha as the child being observed.

When using checklists, teachers can easily gather a great deal of quantifiable data; however, those data lacks the detail of the narrative observation. An effective checklist is dependent on the quality of the items. Often, checklist items are ambiguous or include two different criteria in one item (e.g., child is happy and friendly at school). Therefore, teachers will be most successful when they customize the items to be targeted and specific to their needs. As with all observation recording methods, repeated observations in varying contexts and times of the day provide a more thorough picture.

Two variations of the checklist are frequency counts and duration records (Bentzen, 2001). The frequency count tallies how often the behavior occurs, while the duration record notes the length or extent of the behavior. Mrs. Korn might use a frequency count to track how often Samantha engages in positive and negative interactions with her peers after she operationally defines these behaviors. She would select three intervals during the day to collect her data. Figure 3.3 is an example of Mrs. Korn's frequency count of Samantha's peer interactions.

Rating Scales

Rating scales are yet another method of recording observations. Also known as a Likert scale (Rea & Parker, 1997), rating scales qualify observed behavior by assigning a number value. Typically, rating scales categorize behavior according to a 5-, 7-, or 9-point system. The *Early Childhood Environment Rating Scale* (Harms, Clifford, & Cryer, 2005) is an example of a clear and thorough rating system, although it does not focus on child behavior. As with the checklist, the items are predetermined, making the recording of observations relatively quick and simple. See Figure 3.4 for an example of a peer-interaction rating scale.

Time Sampling and Event Sampling

There are two additional techniques that enable observers to be more efficient in their data collection: time sampling and event sampling (Bentzen, 2001). Both time-sampling and event-sampling methods can be used in conjunction with narratives, checklists, rating scales, and frequency counts. With

Figure 3.2. Peer Interaction Checklist

Name of Student <u>Samantha</u>   **Grade/Class** <u>3-B</u>

Date of Observation <u>12/4/01</u>   **Observer** <u>Mrs. Korn</u>

Setting
This observation takes place in the classroom during group-work time on rain forest animals.
There are three other children in Samantha's group.

Overall Behavior	Observed	Not Observed	N/A
Child typically engages in positive interactions with peers.		√	
Child has developed appropriate and meaningful relationships with peers.		√	
Child demonstrates tolerance when mildly provoked.		√	

Comments
Samantha easily engages with her peers. She annoys Robert and Joe.

Small Groups Within Classroom	Observed	Not Observed	N/A
Child expresses ideas clearly to peers.		√	
Child demonstrates ability to listen to peers.		√	
Child compromises as needed for the group process.		√	

Comments
Samantha has trouble sharing her ideas and listening to others.

Unstructured Periods (Lunch, Recess, Snack Time, Transitions)	Observed	Not Observed	N/A
Child finds a place within a group.			√
Child refrains from following those who are misbehaving.			√
Child possesses ability to resolve conflicts peacefully.			√

Comments
Although this observation does not focus on unstructured activities, I know from past experience
that Samantha has great difficulties during these times.

a time-sampling method, observers set the recording times and intervals for all observations beforehand. For example, a teacher might decide to record observations once a week for 15 minutes. The time of observations can be established (e.g., every Wednesday from 1:00 to 1:15 p.m.) or carried out randomly. Event sampling involves selecting a particular behavior, event, or academic subject to observe and then only recording data during those occasions. Observers must define what that event or behavior is in order to be consistent. Mrs. Korn's recording of Samantha's behavior presented earlier in the narrative, checklist, frequency count, and rating scales are actually event-sampling observations. The focus of each of these observations was specific and only included Samantha's interactions and relationships with peers. They did not describe her cognitive, language, or physical development.

Anecdotes

Yet another observational tool frequently used by teachers is the anecdote (Bentzen, 2001). Anecdotes are a favorite choice because behaviors do not have to be recorded as they occur. Teachers can jot down an observed behavior at the end of the day, during a special, or whenever they get a free moment. Anecdotes are short snippets of events that the teacher has determined are worth documenting. There is tremendous variation involved in the subject and length of observations, but teachers may opt to refine their focus as indicated. Most teachers using anecdotes keep a filing system to easily retrieve observations collected earlier. While there are no necessary guidelines for anecdotes, these observations will be more meaningful later on if they are dated, if they include a context de-

Figure 3.3. Peer Interaction Frequency Count

Name of Student <u>Samantha</u>   Grade/Class <u>3-B</u>

Date of Observation <u>12/4/01</u>   Observer <u>Mrs. Korn</u>

Positive Interaction with Peers

- initiates positive interaction with peers
- responds when approached by other children
- cooperates in group activity

Negative Interaction with Peers

- uses words to hurt
- is physically aggressive
- disrupts others

Positive Interactions with Peers	Negative Interactions with Peers
√√√	√√√√√ √√√√√ √√

Recommendations

During the course of this observation, Samantha repeatedly engaged in negative behavior. This sample is typical of Samantha's ongoing behavior. She's got a big problem, and I need some additional help from the administration. I think she needs psychological counseling.

Figure 3.4. Peer Interaction Rating Scale

Name of Student <u>Samantha</u>   Grade/Class <u>3-B</u>

Date of Observation <u>12/4/01</u>   Observer <u>Mrs. Korn</u>

Directions: Rate each item on a scale of 1–5

1 = never 2 = rarely 3 = sometimes 4 = often 5 = always

- -

Overall Behavior

Child typically engages in positive interactions with peers.

     1   ②   3   4   5

Child has developed appropriate and meaningful relationships with peers.

     ①   2   3   4   5

Child demonstrates tolerance when mildly provoked.

     1   ②   3   4   5

Small Groups Within Classroom

Child expresses ideas clearly to peers.

     1   2   ③   4   5

Child demonstrates ability to listen to peers.

     1   2   ③   4   5

Child compromises as needed for the group process.

     1   ②   3   4   5

Unstructured Periods (Lunch, Recess, Snack Time, Transitions)

Child finds a place within a group.

     1   ②   3   4   5

Child refrains from following those who are misbehaving.

     1   2   3   ④   5

Child has ability to resolve conflicts peacefully and effectively.

     1   ②   3   4   5

- -

Summary of Results

Based on what I saw during this observation, Samantha has tremendous difficulty interacting with her peers. Her inability to compromise, resolve conflicts, and work in a group interferes with her learning. So much of our class time is spent in groups. Most worrisome is her inability to connect with other children. She doesn't have any friends. We need to bring her parents in right away.

---

scription, and if observed behavior is distinguished from inferences. Figure 3.5 presents two anecdotes written by Mrs. Korn. The improvement of the first version is shown in the second version, in which Mrs. Korn's objective observations are separated from her subjective inferences. She also included suggestions for intervention.

OBSERVATIONAL ERRORS

Whichever observational method is chosen, errors are inevitable. The three most common observational errors are omission, commission, and transmission (Bentzen, 2001). With omission, the observer leaves out important information. In commission, the observer elaborates on what is believed to have been seen, making assumptions on the data. For example, it may be assumed that a child who is walking over to the window is intending to look outside. However, the child's real intention was to pass a note to a friend who is sitting near the window. Finally, in transmission, there is an incorrect sequencing of events when the observation is reconstructed and the actual facts are lost.

Issues such as rater bias and inferential and emotionally based observations have already been addressed but present ongoing questions for the observer. Making rash conclusions and taking observations out of context are additional problems that compromise the accuracy of the information that has been gathered. An outsider who walks

Figure 3.5. Anecdotes

Version 1
12/4/01
Re: Samantha

Samantha's difficulties in getting along with her class-mates were highlighted for me today during small-group work on rain forest animal research. Samantha is in a group with Joe, Robert, and Amanda. As most of the students were happily engaged, Samantha was purposefully loud and disruptive not only to her group, but to the class as well. She refused to cooperate with her group and kept bothering me to help her. Samantha clearly shows that she is impulsive, self-centered, and unable to compromise. It should be noted that Amanda, Joe, and Robert demonstrated little tolerance for Samantha's behavior. While they got along just fine with one another, they seem to have reached their limit with Samantha.

Version 2
12/4/01
Re: Samantha

Observations

I observed Samantha today during small-group work on rain forest animal research. Samantha is in a group with Joe, Robert, and Amanda. As most of the students were on task, Samantha was loud and disruptive not only to her group, but to the class as well. She did not cooperate with her group and kept coming up to me for help.

Inferences

Samantha clearly shows that she is impulsive, self-centered, and unable to compromise. It should be noted that Amanda, Joe, and Robert demonstrated little tolerance for Samantha's behavior. While they got along just fine with one another, they seem to have reached their limit with Samantha.

Recommendations

I certainly want to consider putting Samantha in a different group next time to see if there are any children she can get along with. In the meantime, I will keep a close eye on Samantha and keep her within arm's reach. Perhaps I can sit in on her group next time and coach her through the group process. I will also write a note home to let her parents know of my concerns.

into the classroom and sees a behavior without prior knowledge of the child or situation may make certain judgments that are incorrect. Taking into account cultural differences between the observer and the child who is being observed is central to understanding behavior and is another area where mistakes are apt to occur. Insufficient planning, whereby the observer does not have a clear focus on what is to be looked at, may create too wide a lens, leaving in superfluous data. Similarly, having too narrow a focus may bias the observation unnecessarily.

Issues of confidentiality can also be extremely difficult in a setting where professionals live in the same communities as the schoolchildren. Stairways, hallways, supermarkets, and other public places are not venues in which observations and other personal information are shared. A family's privacy must be respected at all costs.

SUPERVISORY ISSUES

Interpersonal relationships between faculty, administration, and families can have an impact on the social dynamics within a classroom. Disagreements about disciplinary practice are inevitable given differences in perspectives, values, and philosophy. Not only do parents and teachers often have distinct expectations for children's behavior, but their responses to misbehavior may also be inconsistent.

Mr. Anderson has worked as a first-grade teacher in his current school for more than 15 years. He has gained a reputation for being organized, creative, humorous, and a tough disciplinarian. Mr. Anderson proudly articulates that he is able to "whip kids into shape" and has said to his students on numerous occasions that he will "ship them out "or "hang them by their britches" if they do not fall into line. Several children apparently take Mr. Anderson's comments literally and have gone home upset. Some parents have called the principal, Dr. Stone, to complain about Mr. Anderson over past few months.

Dr. Stone could handle this dilemma in a number of ways. She could simply inform Mr. Anderson that there have been phone calls from parents and that he is advised to watch his words more carefully. Given the fact that Dr. Stone is new to the school, she might choose to refrain from sharing this information with the hope that these were isolated incidents. After all, Mr. Anderson is a seasoned and well-respected teacher. A more effective strategy would be for Dr. Stone to observe in the classroom to learn more about Mr. Anderson's style of teaching. Ideally, she would meet with

Mr. Anderson periodically, as she does with all the teachers in her school. During such a meeting, Dr. Stone could encourage Mr. Anderson to reflect on his own teaching as a way of recognizing and improving his tone. Dr. Stone might offer direct feedback as well as recommend self-observation for Mr. Anderson, because self-discovery can be a powerful learning tool (Glickman, 2002). Given Mr. Anderson's years of experience and his excellent teaching record, an effective strategy is to encourage him to take the lead in his own supervision. Empowering a teacher to be a researcher, to investigate and then reflect on his own teaching and interactions, is a component of action research (Hobson, 1996).

SELF-ASSESSMENT

The Teacher Self-Reflection Inventory (see Appendix D) helps teachers assess their tone, language, relationships with children, and classroom-management skills. The items on the inventory highlight characteristics of teachers who practice developmental discipline. Although self-assessment is subjective by nature, the inventory can remind teachers about what constitutes good practice. By answering the questions as honestly as possible, teachers identify their own strengths and weaknesses. The inventory is particularly useful for teachers who work in schools without common planning time and ongoing administrative supervision. If Mr. Anderson were to complete a Teacher Self-Reflection Inventory, he might discover that he has a tendency to use sarcasm and scare tactics to manage classroom behavior. Mr. Anderson might realize that his humor, while appreciated by some, confuses and even intimidates others. That was never his intent.

In many cases, teachers become defensive when they deem an evaluation as critical of them. However, when individuals are asked to critique themselves, they tend to be more honest and, if anything, overly critical. A self-reflective inventory can provide an opportunity for genuine self-appraisal. The Teacher Self-Reflection Inventory may be used independently or in the context of a supervisory meeting. Figure 3.6 shows an inventory as it might have been completed by Mr. Anderson.

Other independent strategies for self-reflection are journaling and videotaping oneself. An ongoing journal in which teachers note their innermost feelings can very useful in illuminating problems. Without a venue for expressing one's discontent, anger, and frustrations, a teacher's practice becomes impaired. Personal insights gleaned from journal entries can contribute to identifying and solving problems. Ideally, a teacher would share revelations with a colleague who can offer objective guidance. Teacher support or supervisory groups can use journaling as a basis for discussion. For those teachers who lack collegial assistance, journals can provide a window into patterns and challenges that require attention. Videotaping, too, can be a powerful tool for examining one's own practice.

A similar form, the Student Self-Reflection Inventory (see Appendix E) is useful in helping older students, perhaps 8 years and up, to engage in self-observation. The primary goal of this inventory is for students to become cognizant of their own behavior and then take responsibility. This inventory can be used preventatively by establishing a baseline for behavior, with at-risk children or with those already exhibiting negative behavior. The Student Self-Reflection Inventory may be administered at several points throughout the year to note improvement or regression in the children's development. Chris, age 9, is frequently reprimanded by his teacher for calling out and disrupting lessons. His teacher asked him to complete a Student Self-Reflection Inventory in the hope that Chris would gain some insight into his behavior. Figure 3.7 is presented to show what Chris's inventory might look like.

In many instances, children blame others when they "get in trouble" and do not see how they actually regulate their own actions. Teachers may try to control children's behavior, usually with unsuccessful results. This is simply because one cannot control another—adults cannot control young children. Teachers can, however, guide and teach appropriate behavior and help instill a sense of self-control and accountability. The Student Self-Reflection Inventory conveys to children that they are capable of looking inward and monitoring themselves. Adults can encourage children to fill out the form either independently or with assistance. In both cases, the child would work with a

Figure 3.6. Teacher Self-Reflection Inventory

Name <u>John Anderson</u>   **Date of Observation** <u>March 17, 2004</u>

Directions: Rate each item. Think about one or two examples to support each answer.

1 = never   2 = rarely   3 = sometimes   4 = often   5 = always

- -

Tone

My tone is positive and nonthreatening.

        1   2   3   ④   5

I modulate my voice as a teaching tool.

        1   2   3   4   ⑤

My students understand my humor.

        1   2   ③   4   5

Comments

When it comes to my humor, I tend to interject old-fashioned expressions that the kids don't always get. I don't want to treat them as babies, so I don't talk down to them. But some kids can be overly sensitive.

Language

My students understand my vocabulary and the way I use language.

        1   2   ③   4   5

I state my expectations clearly.

        1   2   3   4   ⑤

I individualize my responses to each child.

        1   2   ③   4   5

Comments

I think I do a very good job of individualizing the curriculum to match my kids' abilities. Maybe I could be more sensitive to how some kids are going to interpret what I say.

Relationships with Children

I establish relationships with the children in my class.

        1   2   3   ④   5

I look at children's faces and body language to gauge their reactions.

        1   2   3   ④   5

I use active listening skills with the children.

        1   2   3   ④   5

Comments

I typically connect well with my students. Most kids seem to really like me. I suppose there are some kids every year that seem to keep their distance from me. Maybe I can be a little intimidating.

Classroom Management Skills

I clarify classroom rules and expectations on a regular basis.

        1   2   3   4   ⑤

I respond consistently with logical consequences.

        1   2   3   ④   5

I encourage the children to communicate and problem solve.

        1   2   3   ④   5

Comments

Behavior management is not a problem in my class. They know what they're supposed to do. I know I'm firm, but do I come on too strong?

- -

Reflections and Goals

When I seriously reflect, I recognize that my tone and expressions can be confusing and upsetting to some children. I know I'm a good teacher, an excellent teacher, really, but sometimes I should be more warm and fuzzy. My goal for the rest of the school year is to be more cognizant of my students' developmental levels and sensitivities. I will try to adjust my words accordingly.

---

teacher to explore some of the issues that are raised and to develop strategies for improvement.

CONCLUSION

Regardless of the method, observation is a critical piece of behavior management in school. Observation helps to pinpoint the motivation behind the behavior, thus enabling a plan of action to be implemented that relates specifically to the child and situation. Discipline often fails when teachers do not sufficiently understand the reasons for the misbehavior and the interventions are not specifically targeted. There are no universal discipline methods. In a later chapter, misused discipline strategies such as time-out, forced apologies, and sending children to the principal's office will be discussed. It is through observation that educators can go beyond behavior to truly understand children and to effect positive change at school. On the basis of this chapter, we

Figure 3.7. Student Self-Reflection Inventory

Name <u>Chris</u>   Date <u>Nov. 4</u>

Directions: Rate each item as 1, 2, or 3. Think about one or two examples
to support each answer.

1 = rarely   2 = sometimes   3 = usually

- -

I am good at following rules in

Class

①   2   3

Specials

1   ②   3

Hallways

①   2   3

Lunch and recess

1   ②   3

I am a good listener

In small group work

1   ②   3

When my teacher is teaching

①   2   3

With my friends

1   2   ③

I am respectful to my

Teachers

①   2   3

Classmates

1   2   ③

Other adults in school

1   ②   3

- -

Complete the following

I get in trouble because

my teacher doesn't like me. She's always yelling at me just because I'm talking to my friends.
School is so boring anyway.

I could do a better job in school by

not getting into trouble all the time.

My friends like me because

they think I'm cool.

Something important to know about me is

I don't always like getting into trouble. I wish my teacher liked me.

---

encourage teachers to consider the following
recommendations:

- Use the observational process: planning, objective observation/documentation, assessment/recommendations, and intervention/follow-up

- Formally observe using one or a combination of recording methods
- Differentiate between objective observation and subjective inference to minimize bias
- Engage in self-reflection
- Help students self-reflect on their own behavior

CHAPTER 4

Challenges in the First 3 Years

Eight-month-old Jasmine sits on the lap of Sandra, her caregiver, and babbles happily. Jasmine leans forward, grabs Sandra's glasses, and throws them on the floor, for the third time. Sandra smiles as she retrieves them, places them back on, and thinks to herself that this is annoying behavior. Jasmine then slaps Sandra in the face, and Sandra laughingly says to Jasmine, "No." Undeterred, Jasmine lifts her hand to hit her caregiver again.

Developmental discipline begins in infancy and continues through toddlerhood, with parents and teachers/caregivers helping children establish positive behavior patterns. A child's age determines the appropriateness and response to behaviors, but it is never too early to establish rules. In fact, the later one starts to define limits and boundaries, the more difficult they are to enforce. Clearly, the caregiver in this vignette did not seriously attempt to curtail the child's negative behavior. While it is developmentally appropriate for Jasmine to explore and test her caregiver, it is not acceptable to slap, bite, or hurt others in any way, and children must learn early on what is permitted. It is not a good idea to allow young children to treat an adult's body or belongings (e.g., glasses, jewelry, paperwork) as playthings.

ROUTINES

Through routines and schedules of infancy including eating, awake time, and sleeping, infants'

ability to regulate their own behavior is initiated. A level of homeostasis is critical for a baby's sense of well-being and essential for later development. Adults observe and read infants' signals to determine their needs and respond accordingly. For example, parents and caregivers learn that when a baby rubs his eyes, or becomes particularly fussy, he may be getting tired. Recognizing those signs and, as a result, instituting daily naps and regular bedtimes creates a safe and familiar environment for the child that is important to maintain both at home and in child care. Although many infants resist going to sleep, often when they need it most, caregivers need to enforce a sleep routine calmly and consistently rather than give in to the resistance. Establishing a routine early on saves parents and caregivers endless hours of power struggle at nap- or bedtime. While occasionally naps may be skipped because of changes in routine, it is best to preserve the consistency of the daily schedule to further demonstrate that parents and the caregivers set the rules in accordance with the child's needs. Many beleaguered parents seek out the advice of sleep experts such as Ferber (1986), who helps parents to retrain their infants and toddlers to develop healthy sleep habits. However, it is exceedingly difficult to break bad habits or patterns that have already been formed.

Meal- and snack time are other opportunities for adults to observe and intervene when necessary. Infants explore their meals as part of learning about the various dimensions in the world—tastes, smells, and textures. However, after an infant dumps her food toward the end of a meal or deliberately makes a mess, parents and caregivers learn through observation to anticipate this behavior and react accordingly. Food may be removed, or the baby may be taken away from the table, to reinforce that throwing food is not acceptable. A toddler who walks around the house with food or who returns to the table asking for more when the meal has clearly ended is exhibiting behavior that could be modified with clear and consistent messages. When instructed in this manner, very young children learn over time what to expect from parents and caregivers and what behaviors are expected of them.

The Importance of Limit Setting

Certainly, adults' demands about behavior in infancy and toddlerhood need to be realistic and based on developmental norms and individual temperament. Toddlers have their own unique timetable for acquiring the skills necessary for potty learning (aka toilet training), which can certainly exasperate parents and caregivers alike. Using the toilet appropriately depends on developmental readiness: cognitive understanding, the ability to communicate, as well as physical maturity. Adults cannot dictate this milestone because it is ultimately within the control of young children. Yet children often use this control (and their parents' desperation for this milestone to be achieved) to test limits and frustrate adults. Testing of limits is an important task in growing up. In the realm of potty learning, it is far more beneficial to be patient and relaxed during the process and convey a sense of confidence to children that they will achieve this skill in due time.

Parents and teachers will understandably set their own rules about what behavior is reasonable. This is culturally determined as different priorities and time lines are placed on the achievement of these milestones. For example, in Chinese societies parents may begin to toilet train their babies at 6 months of age (Huntsinger, Huntsinger, Ching, & Lee, 2000). Whatever the family's values or cultural viewpoints, adults take the lead role in shaping behavior. However, ideally the child's individual needs and developmental timetable would be taken into consideration.

Limit setting, begun during these critical early months, defines for children what is and is not acceptable behavior. Initially, adults establish restrictions externally, and then, over time, children

incorporate them into their own behavioral repertoire. This progression is observed when parents warn their babies to stay away from the stove, stating loudly and clearly, "No, hot!" Over time, toddlers will recite the "No, hot" warnings as they approach the stove until they no longer need to verbally remind themselves of the danger.

Typically, adults are exceedingly clear about limits regarding dangerous situations that may affect children's safety; they do it instinctively. However, they are far less definitive when it comes to establishing disciplinary rules and boundaries over less serious infractions, which, in the long run, have significant ramifications for behavior. In the earlier vignette, Jasmine should have been told firmly and clearly that glasses are not for playing with. While the words may not be entirely understood, a strong tone coupled with a stern face would have shown Jasmine that her caregiver was adamant about stopping the behavior. Sandra might have also responded by removing Jasmine from her lap with another clear message that "we don't hit." Her laughter sent a mixed message to Jasmine that throwing glasses and hitting were actually acceptable and perhaps even enjoyable. Saying no without a reinforcing nonverbal response to a child of this age compromised the clarity of the communication. With infants, toddlers, and young children, the corrective message usually needs to be repeated. Sandra needs to be consistent and patient until she notices the desired outcome, as Jasmine may initially test Sandra's persistence.

Adult Beliefs About Discipline

Parents and teachers must observe and pay careful attention to their own verbal and nonverbal responses to determine if their actions are supporting their words. Sandra might ask herself reflective questions about Jasmine's behavior as well as her own:

- Is Jasmine's playfulness always accompanied by some aggression?
- Could Sandra possibly elicit or reinforce Jasmine's response with her laughter?
- Does Jasmine become easily frustrated or angry?
- Is she more likely to behave in this manner when she is getting tired or hungry?

Answering these questions along with frequent observations of Jasmine and her "playfulness" might yield significant information that would help her caregiver tune in more effectively to her behavior.

Adults also need to consider whether their disciplinary responses vary with gender. Some who adhere to the age-old myth that "boys will be boys" may be more tolerant of boys' aggressive behavior. Others may be especially harsh with boys in an effort to toughen them up. There are diverse attitudes within cultures about whether crying in boys may be sanctioned or forbidden (Pollack, 1998). Additionally, parents and teachers may be excessively lenient with girls and unable to say no to them because they are "so cute." In contrast, adults may attempt to extinguish aggressive behavior that may be seen as unladylike.

Adults' belief systems determine in part their interactive styles with children. Some feelings are latent, while others are manifest. Favoritism of one gender over another may be observed. Becoming cognizant of gender-based attitudes can help parents and educators gain more insight into their actions. This can be accomplished by considering the reasons for past responses and anticipating future interactions.

If Sandra were to consider all the above-mentioned factors—verbal and nonverbal communication, gender, culture, temperament, and so forth—she would discover the relationship between her caregiving style and Jasmine's behavior. Bouncing ideas off of a colleague would additionally provide Sandra with a fresh perspective on the situation. These insights gained from personal introspection and professional feedback will direct Sandra to the changes she needs to make. Sustained change in children's behavior only occurs when adults are willing to modify their own behavior.

THE CHILD WHO BITES

Olivia is an 18-month-old attending child care. She is in the dramatic-play area, with three other children, where there is little room and only a few props. After being bumped by another child, Olivia bites him on the arm. Olivia's teacher, who is frustrated by Olivia's frequent biting, implements her usual strategy by immediately going over and asking why she did it. When Olivia does not answer, the teacher provides her with a lengthy and elaborate explanation of why biting is wrong. Olivia begins to cry.

Educators who have observed children biting may relate to this teacher's frustration. While the teacher's response to Olivia's behavior may have been with the best of intentions, the outcome of the intervention was not successful, as demonstrated by the repeated biting. It is normal for negative behavior to continue despite an adult's attempts to extinguish it. Children persevere for many reasons, including willfulness and a lack of understanding. Through observation, a teacher can ascertain whether a child is testing limits or has not yet internalized the expectations. The teacher decides if repetition of the correction is sufficient to influence the child or if a modification in the intervention is warranted. Educators must be flexible in their approach and alter their procedure if they determine that the effort is not working over time. It is recommended that parents and teachers review the observation process and change their responses to best address the negative behavior.

Biting can be very disruptive to the mood and morale of an early childhood program. There may be isolated incidences, a repeat biter, or contagion within the environment. When early childhood programs group children according to their age, as is typically found in child-care centers, biting can be especially problematic because there are several children at the "biting age." With mixed-aged grouping, biting epidemics may be less prevalent (Balaban, 1991).

Whether occurrences are frequent or occasional, biting upsets not only the children who are most likely to be the victims, but also the adults who are responsible for their care. Adults, too, play a large role in the drama that unfolds after a biting scenario, when the parents of the other children in the classroom demand that the biter be removed from the program. Too often, toddlers are asked to leave their playgroups or child care because the caregivers do not know how to stop the problem. Biting can be regarded as abnormal or primitive even in young children, resulting in negative perceptions about the child. Therefore adults' responses to biting may be emotionally driven rather than rational.

When addressing biting behavior, it is essential to consider the child's age, individual developmental level, temperament, and other behavioral or situational factors. Biting in toddlers and 2-year-olds who lack sufficient verbal skills is common and to be expected. After all, their verbal abilities do not necessarily match their cognitive abilities, and this mismatch often leads to frustration. Anticipating that toddlers may bite, especially when the behavior has been observed previously, is crucial. Challenging behavior such as biting, often regarded as deviant, can instead be reframed as a developmentally appropriate response when one lacks the ability to verbally communicate.

While it is not unusual for adults to ask young children the reasons for their actions, it is not possible for a child of Olivia's age to fully articulate her motives. Even if she were able to reflect, which in itself is highly unlikely, she would not yet have the vocabulary to explain her feelings, such as anger, frustration, fatigue, jealousy, and so forth. Therefore, asking a preverbal or semiverbal child why he or she did something wrong is ineffective. If Olivia were older, asking her why she hurt another child would be problematic as it might give her reason to believe that her behavior could be justified. Children are quick to blame others for their aggressive actions, and adults feed into this pattern by asking them why they hit, pushed, or bit. Young children need to learn that despite situations being unfair or another child's wronging them first, hurting another person is not acceptable.

At the same time, knowing a child's reasons or motivations for inappropriate behavior is necessary for effective intervention. When parents and teachers understand the precipitating factors or situational variables that trigger biting, they can anticipate and then prevent it through distraction or redirection. Children bite for many reasons: some intentionally to hurt and others because they are ignorant of its effect. Infants and toddlers sometimes bite when they are teething and seek relief for their aching gums. Some children bite when they are hungry, tired, overstimulated, frustrated, bored, or angry. Still others become overly enthusiastic in their affection, possibly literally interpreting their parents' loving statement "I'm going to eat you up," and their kisses turn into bites. Children may

bite in crowded environments, during activities that require sharing, with certain peers, or at a particular of time of day: prior to naptime, during transitions, or at pickup time.

Understanding the reasons for biting influences the response. For example, a teething child may need to chew an apple or an angry child might benefit from open-ended art, music, or movement activities. A child who bites to seek attention from adults might stop when provided with ample positive interpersonal experiences.

For many children who are chronic biters, having an adult within arm's reach during a biting phase is often the best solution. When a child is reprimanded for biting, it is only after the episode has occurred, when the child has already received oral gratification as well as negative attention. Shadowing the child helps to anticipate the behavior and provides a reassuring presence that assists the child in behaving appropriately. Stopping the child before she is successful, and then providing the simple reminder that biting is not OK along with her removal from the situation, is usually the most effective strategy. It takes a positive attitude, commitment, and patience, but the child soon learns that biting will not be tolerated. Early childhood teachers are quick to point out that shadowing is not very practical, considering they have other children to care for. Yet the "shadower," or adult providing additional attention to a child who bites, is still accessible to the other children. The adult simply positions herself adjacent to the child, ready to place a hand on a shoulder, while continuing to observe and interact with the rest of the children in the program.

Olivia's teacher could best help her by observing and documenting her behavior, thus learning the circumstances in which the behavior typically occurs. Additionally, she would self-reflect to assess if her strategy matched Olivia's needs. In this scenario, an overcrowded play area with too few attractive materials coupled with a child with a history of biting is a risky combination and could be avoided with good planning based on thoughtful observation.

If the teacher were to look carefully, it would be apparent that Olivia was not learning from her lecture. Toddlers (and older children as well) often tune out adults when they are presented with a long, complicated explanation of why their behavior was wrong. Children have limited attention spans, and their capacity to listen is further affected by the content of the message. When it is necessary to correct behavior, it is much more effective to look directly at the child, provide a firm and concise, "No! You may not bite!" and subsequently remove the child from the situation.

TANTRUMS

Biting is just one challenging behavior that can be observed in the first 3 years of a child's life. When any difficult behavior is understood within the context of normal development, the adults' response to the child can facilitate a more rapid progression through the phase. Adults who react with excessive frustration and anger toward a child can inadvertently cause the behavior to take on a new significance. Temper tantrums, for example, can be overwhelming, especially if the adult believes that the child is being purposely defiant or disrespectful. In fact, temper tantrums are a developmentally appropriate coping strategy and typical for toddlers, though not adaptive over time (Zeitlin, Williamson, & Szczepanski, 1988). Initially, tantrums serve as a mechanism for a child to let off stream or express dissatisfaction with a situation, particularly if he lacks the social and communication skills to express himself adequately. A 2-year-might throw himself on the floor of the playroom, kicking and screaming, when told that he cannot have the toy he wants. Without the child's having the cognitive ability to comprehend why his teacher said no, and without the verbal skills to express his feelings and desires, the tantrum relieves the child of his tensions and frustrations and simultaneously sends a strong message to his teacher. Likewise, a 14-month-old learns fairly quickly that her loud, wild cries cause adults to stop whatever they are doing to tend to her. Tantrums become integrated into her behavioral pattern because they are successful in getting attention.

When the adult counters a tantrum with reprimands or by giving in to the child's demands, the behavior is reinforced and likely to reoccur. Trying to reason with a child who is out of control and emotionally volatile will also not be successful because he is unable to hear and process what is being said. Expecting a child to just snap out of a tantrum is not realistic developmentally. When

tantrums are ignored, however, they tend to dissipate over time. Children learn that temper tantrums are not an effective means of getting attention or what they want. Adults can, at the same time, communicate their recognition of the child's feelings and the belief that the child can and will be able to calm down. Additionally, the adult can reassure the child that he will be there if needed, whenever the tantrum ends.

SHARING AND TURN TAKING

Sharing is a domain in which adults' expectations are not necessary commensurate with children's developmental level. In child-care programs and schools, teachers insist that children share toys, equipment, and materials. It is not unusual for a child to grab one toy and say, "Mine." A teacher will typically answer, "No, that toy is not yours. It belongs to everyone, and you have to share." The child who claimed the toy was hers did not mean to indicate that she had actually purchased the item and was legally entitled to possess it. Instead, she meant that she had it at that moment; the toy was in her hands. Children are placed in group environments for several hours a day, perhaps most of their waking time, and told that nothing is theirs. It is no wonder that children in this situation react negatively to forced sharing.

Sharing is a culturally based concept, not just a behavior. Americans are raised to be independent, think for themselves, and meet their own needs. They are taught to strive to be the best, to be number one, and as a result often acquire a sense of entitlement. In many families, members have their own bedrooms, bathrooms, telephones, televisions, cars, and so forth. It is ironic that adults expect children to share their toys when they themselves model the opposite behavior.

In some families, children live in poverty; food, clothing, and toys are scarce, and everything must be shared. These children may have no possessions that are entirely their own. Expecting those children to readily share materials in school to which they have little access at home may be too much to ask.

If sharing is a value that adults wish to instill, and not just a logistical tool for managing a group of children, then they must recognize that the ability to do so must correspond with the child's understanding of why it is important. Developing a community of sharing evolves slowly over time with concerted effort and consistent expectations. It is interesting to watch children who are not forced to share toys. They tend to gravitate toward that behavior instinctively, as an expression of their innate social disposition.

When faced with the dilemma of two children desiring the same toy at the same time, it is always preferable to allow children time with the toy alone, thus entitling each one to own the toy for a limited period of time. Taking turns, perhaps with the help of a clock or egg timer, is a dramatically different approach to forced sharing. While playing independently may be enjoyable for a time, many children will choose the company of others, thus creating situations in which the willingness to share is necessary. However, some children will more often than not prefer to play by themselves, perhaps because of their temperament or upbringing. Teachers must respect those individual differences and needs. Providing sharing opportunities that are inevitable in a classroom environment, and modeling sharing behavior, are more subtle ways to encourage a reluctant child. Forced sharing will have a limited benefit because it will not take place spontaneously without an adult present.

SLEEPING ISSUES

Two-year-old David is having trouble falling asleep at naptime in his child-care center. He starts on his own cot with his caregiver, Julie, rubbing his back, but as soon as she moves to another child, David is up and moving around. He is told by Julie to lie quietly, but instead David talks aloud and rattles his cot. Julie returns to soothe David, but as soon as she leaves, David begins to cry and disturb the other children. She reluctantly sits next to him until he eventually falls asleep. This pattern has been in place since David started child care one year ago.

Sleep disturbances in children are a ubiquitous concern among adults who spend hours walking, rocking, and comforting young children to help them fall asleep. There is a great deal of variability in the age in which children fall asleep on their own, and this benchmark is often considered a definition of a "good baby." Sleep/wake time in children varies tremendously based on age, physiology, temperament, and environment. Characteristics of parents also have an impact on children's sleeping behavior. Depression, anxiety, and stress have been noted in parents of children who have sleep difficulties (Godfrey, 1998). What is often overlooked is the adults' role in establishing clear limits and routines that facilitate a child's ability to go to sleep and stay asleep.

By 4 months, a child should have a relatively stable sleep routine (Brazelton, 1992). However, David, even by age 2, does not have a particularly adaptive sleep routine at child care. He continues to manipulate the caregiver to the point that she must be next to him in order for him to settle down. He remains vigilant to her whereabouts, rather than allowing himself to relax and fall asleep. When Julie attempts to leave after a significant amount of time spent engaged in their prolonged "sleep ritual," he pops up again and demands attention. Frustrated, she acquiesces and rewards him with her continued presence.

If Julie were to step back and observe the pattern that existed, she might learn the precipitating factors contributing to David's sleeping habits. David may only have difficulties at naptime in child care but have little trouble going to sleep at home. It is extremely hard for children to let go of the excitement of the day, and as a result they often prolong the experience by demanding the presence of their caregivers, even in the face of increased exhaustion. This is particularly true at child care, where activities are stimulating and there are peers with whom to engage. Because naptime is usually scheduled after lunch for all children, David may simply not be ready to go to sleep at this time. Some children may not need to nap and thus may find the scheduled rest period frustrating and unduly restrictive.

Changes in routine, an illness, or a stressful home environment may also have a negative impact on David's overall sleep pattern. Periodic sleep disturbances may be related to new skills and cognitive abilities in the developing toddler. Overstimulating environments, even at naptime, can make it hard for some children to unwind, particularly if they are experiencing sensory-integration issues. Through her observations, Julie can evaluate David's unique circumstances and determine what would be most beneficial to establish a positive and consistent sleep routine. Communicating with David's parents to learn about his sleep habits at home and their expectations about naptime in child care is also necessary. Cultural differences and their influences on sleep routines should be considered. North American and Western European expectations that children sleep in their own crib and eventually their own bed often clashes with customs in other cultures in which "co-sleeping" is preferred (Minde, 1998). Teachers must use caution and refrain from being ethnocentric.

Julie might begin her observations by focusing on the time period before naptime to better understand David's functioning within his environment. She would specifically look at how he anticipates and handles transitions. At the same time, Julie needs to think about how she and her colleagues prepare children for naptime. A narrative observation, such as shown in Figure 4.1, is indicated, as it would yield a substantial amount of qualitative information. Observations during this time are undoubtedly challenging, requiring multitasking on the part of the teachers. Yet this process is necessary in order to figure out exactly what is going on with David. Once his needs are ascertained, the teachers can then modify the environment, change the routine, or alter their own interactions to achieve the desired results. This is not easy, as teachers still have a classroom to maintain.

In many cases creating an individual "going-to-sleep ritual" may result in children's ability to go to sleep on their own. Naptime rituals may consist of a special song; a story; a calming sequence of activities; or a unique activity with a particular child, such as snuggling or rocking in a chair. However, remaining with the toddler for the duration of naptime is not practical. Agreeing to excessive demands in order to placate a child who is reluctant to go to sleep only feeds into that child's belief that he is in control. Adults must draw their line in the sand and communicate that boundary effectively and sincerely. This process may be complex and take several days or even weeks to put into effect. Caregivers need to cope with those challenging naptimes when children will inevitably resist

Figure 4.1. Narrative Observation

Observer <u>Julie</u>　　　　Date <u>11/4/04</u>

Child's Name <u>David</u>　　Child's Age <u>26 months</u>

Context:

　Physical Setting: This is a typical child-care class. There are play areas, tables and chairs, a changing table with a couple of potties nearby. When the 12 cots are set up, the room is quite crowded.

　Situation: We've just finished lunch. The room is a mess, and the kids are running around. There are 12 toddlers in the room with Anna and me. We're trying to clean them up, change their diapers, and get them ready for naptime.

Time	Behavioral Descriptions (objective)	Interpretations/Inferences (subjective)
12:30 p.m.	David is running around the room with other children. He is repeatedly saying, "Run, run, run" in a loud voice.	David is winding up, not winding down. He's having a good time. I wish I could calm him down, but I'm busy changing diapers.
12:32	David runs from me when I approach him to change his diaper. He puts up a struggle when I lift him and place him on the changing table.	David's mood changes as he anticipates naptime. Other than naptime, he does not resist having his diaper changed.
12:40	David is asked to lie down on his cot. He says no and picks up his cot and bangs it down on the floor.	This is typical naptime behavior. How can I better prepare him for napping? How can I make the room less stimulating for him?
12:45	David is told to stop banging his cot because he is disturbing other children, but he continues.	I wonder if it would be possible for me to take David out of the room for quiet while Anna took care of the rest of the kids.

and test the new limits that have been imposed. It is during these moments that children learn that adults are there to take care of them. Over time, they learn that their caregiver will not reward negative behavior.

Depending on what Julie learns from her observations, she may choose to reconfigure the sleeping environment and place David's cot in a cozy corner to minimize excessive noise and contact with other children. Many children in child care benefit from a transitional object, such as a blanket or stuffed animal, to comfort them. Enlisting David's parents in the problem solving is important, to determine the most appropriate interventions for David. Partnering with parents helps to shed light on details that may be missing from the educator's point of view. Parents and teachers can support each other in their efforts to provide the best and most consistent care for young children.

TYPICAL AND ATYPICAL BEHAVIOR

Through observation, coupled with knowledge of child development, adults learn what is typical behavior in children, aged 0 to 3. At the same time, however, behaviors that warrant greater study may be noted. These behaviors may be transient in nature or suggest a more serious developmental problem. They are warning signs and may be called "red-flag behaviors" (see the list in Figure 4.2). It is critical for educators working with this age group to be familiar with those signs of atypical behavior in order to intervene in a timely and appropriate fashion. Parents often yield to the views of educators and depend on them for an objective assessment. Teachers and early childhood administrators are on the front line of early intervention, as they are most likely to detect developmental delays.

Two-and-a-half-year-old Kevin prefers to play by himself in his child-care program. When other children interact with him, he pushes them away. At times, Kevin will unexpectedly scream and throw toys and chairs around the room. When adults attempt to engage Kevin, he averts his eyes and tries to hide under the table or in the corner. Kevin's teachers have shared their observations with the child-care direc-

tor, who in turn has been in constant communication with his parents. The parents report that Kevin has not always behaved in this manner, and they too are worried.

Kevin's behavior is of concern. His solitary behavior, rejection of social overtures by peers and adults, and aggressive outbursts are atypical. Toddlers usually enjoy the camaraderie of others and often seek out teachers for attention and comfort. Kevin's preference for being alone is not necessarily alarming. However, his behavior is part of an ongoing pattern that typifies his functioning in the setting, and apparently at home as well. What is most worrisome is that Kevin has regressed in his social, emotional, and language development.

It is likely that Kevin attracted the attention of his teachers because of his acting-out rather than because of his solitary play, which is not disruptive. Children who are quiet or passive often get overlooked but still require teachers' responsiveness. In this case, Kevin's difficulties were noticed early in his group-care experience. Because of this timely identification, the child-care educators, in tandem with Kevin's parents, can begin an early intervention process.

Working with Families

Information gathering has actually begun, with both Kevin's teachers and parents documenting Kevin's behavior in child care and at home. They noted that Kevin's "meltdowns" tend to occur when demands are made of him to interact with others or transition to a new activity. Rather than respond with words, Kevin vocalizes unintelligible sounds in protest. While the staff has never heard Kevin speak words, his mother reports that Kevin uses some words at home, but in general his verbalizations have decreased.

According to Kevin's parents, his pediatrician did not detect unusual behavior upon exam and tried to reassure them that Kevin was just going through a phase. However, Kevin's deteriorating behavior at home and his poor adaptation to the child-care environment still need to be addressed. Understanding and modifying Kevin's environment is the primary goal of the developmental discipline observation process (see Chap-

Figure 4.2. Red-Flag Behaviors

Birth–3 Years	*3–5 Years (includes all of the above)*
• Poor muscle tone and stability	• Weak fine-motor skills; avoids drawing, cutting, puzzles, etc.
• Jerky or clumsy movement (hypotonic or hypertonic)	• Low energy level
• Hands mostly fisted after 4 months of age	• Hyperactive
• Asymmetry of body and movement; uneven posture	• Absence of spontaneous speech
• Persistent walking on toes	• Does not have extensive vocabulary
• Poor suck or swallow, excessive drool, protruding tongue	• Lack of curiosity; reluctant to explore the environment
• Does not visually track objects or turn toward sounds	• Inability to sustain attention to learning tasks
• Hypersensitivity to stimuli	• Resistant to participating in group activities
• Rocking or other self-stimulating and repetitive behaviors (e.g., flapping, twirling, head banging)	• Difficulty transitioning
• Excessive preoccupation with one toy	• Inability to adapt to routines
• Absence of vocalizations	• Purposeful hurting of people and property
• Echolalia	• Does not make friends
• Unresponsive to people, environment, or both	• Unwilling to take risks
• Flat or no affect	• Fixation on touching genitals and other body parts
• Displays mostly negative affect	*School-Age Children (includes all of the above)*
• Cannot be comforted when upset	• Eating abnormalities
• No eye contact	• Learning difficulties
• Excessive stranger or separation distress	• Unsuccessful academic experiences
• Multiple/excessive fears	• Unwilling to complete school assignments
• Night terrors or repeated nightmares	• Resistance to attending school
• Self-mutilating behaviors	• Excessive school absenteeism and tardiness
• Excessive aggression	• Apathy
• Eating/sleeping disturbances	• Stealing
• Inability to form relationships	• Chronic lying
• Loss of a developmental milestone; regressive behavior	• Bullying and other threatening behavior
	• Shows no remorse
	• Marked changes in behavior
	• Depression or anxiety
	• Provocative language, dress, and sexual gestures
	• Drug and alcohol use

ter 3). This process formally begins when parents, teachers, and the director meet to strategize together. The steps include planning, implementing, documenting objective observations, interpreting those findings, making recommendations about appropriate intervention, and then following through.

Within a few weeks, the team, that is, teachers, administrators, and parents, determined that an outside evaluation for Kevin was warranted. Acknowledging that one does not have all the an-

swers and knowing when to get additional help are important professional moments. Child-care programs and schools can support their teachers by providing in-service workshops addressing the specific difficulties that children present. Whether the program is public or privately funded, it is covered by the federal Individuals with Disabilities Education Act, which mandates that all children are entitled to a free and thorough evaluation and subsequent services if indicated. Some families are reluctant participants in the diagnostic process because navigating through the special-services system can be a daunting challenge. This is especially true for those families who suffer economic hardships, who feel disenfranchised from the school and the community, for whom English is not the first language, or who have had no prior experience advocating for their children. Learning different terminology, accommodating to the timetable of necessary appointments, and following through on the recommendations is not easy. Despite the findings indicating that there is a problem, families may not fully accept that their child has a disability. These are the families who may require hand-holding and additional assistance throughout the various phases of assessment.

In the weeks or months that are required to complete an evaluation, Kevin's teachers and parents need to support one another and work together to help Kevin function in child care and at home. Ideally, the program would solicit the advice of experts through in-service training and outside workshops. When that is not a realistic option because of budgetary constraints, the Internet is an alternative invaluable resource for professional development. Strategies may include instituting a behavior modification program whereby Kevin is rewarded for behaviors such as eye contact, verbalizations, and participation in the group. Using a parent volunteer or the director as a shadow for Kevin during difficult or transition periods can also be effective. Observations will determine when and under what circumstances Kevin would benefit from a nearby adult. Additional information that would be gleaned from systematic observations will reveal activities or situations that must be avoided because they are excessively stimulating. These may include whole-group activities such as circle time. Kevin's apparent need for interpersonal distance must be acknowledged and respected. Therefore, Kevin should have an opportunity to play by himself without the distraction of other children in a particular area. A long-term goal would be to gradually develop his tolerance for being with other children.

Looking at the impact of the physical space on Kevin is necessary. For example, Kevin needs a semiprivate space for some quiet time. Most important, Kevin's teacher must have appropriate expectations of him to enable Kevin to be successful in this inclusive environment. Helping the other children and their parents be sensitive to Kevin's interactive style is an integral element of a caring and nurturing classroom community.

CONCLUSION

One important challenge for educators who work with toddlers is seeing the youngsters' difficult behavior in a more positive light. The expression "terrible twos" reflects the frustration of adults who do not appreciate the importance of defiance and limit testing in young children. The 2nd and 3rd years of life are full of wonderful discoveries, including the sense of the power of the word *no*. Children must establish their autonomy and independence or risk being filled with self-doubt and despair (Erikson, 1963). Teachers need to adjust their lenses and refocus their perceptions of negative behavior. Misbehavior, including acts of aggression, is to be expected along with children's learning to accept the limitations created by adults. This process proceeds more easily when excessive anxiety and concern about children's behavior is minimized. To that end, it is critical for adults to know the difference between difficult phases of normal development and behavior that indicates a more significant problem.

Developmental discipline is an approach that is based on appropriate expectations for both typically and atypically developing children. Initiated early in infancy, it can set a foundation for future behavior. With the use of focused observation to monitor behavior, responses can be tailored to individual children and situations. Adults, too, learn from these observations about their goals, motivations, and effectiveness with the developing child. Reaching out for professional assistance when indicated is also imperative. Developmental discipline is a process from infancy through early childhood and beyond. On the basis of what we discussed in this chapter, we recommend that teachers do the following:

- Be cognizant of typical and atypical development
- Set limits, beginning in infancy

- Observe infants' daily routines to be better attuned to their needs and temperaments
- Recognize that biting and other forms of aggression in infants and toddlers are developmentally appropriate

- Maintain realistic expectations about children's sharing
- Reframe negative behavior in a positive light
- Collaborate with families on observation and problem solving

CHAPTER 5

The Preschooler and Kindergartner

It is the 2nd month of prekindergarten. Kiani is having trouble following the rules in school. She is disruptive during circle time, frequently shouting, "Excuse me," over the voices of the other children and teachers. When her teachers tell her to stop being noisy, she often responds by flailing her arms and legs and crying. Transitions are particularly hard for Kiani, and she periodically stages a "sit-down strike" at the end of an activity. This demonstration may include her crawling under a table, rolling around the floor, sucking her thumb, or making her body rigid, refusing to move. Her teachers are extremely frustrated and spend a great deal of time correcting her negative behaviors. Kiani's grandmother, who shares caregiving with her daughter, states that she is more lenient than her daughter, who punishes Kiani by putting her in her room and letting her cry herself to sleep.

BEGINNING SCHOOL

For 3- and 4-year-olds adapting to a preschool, nursery, child care, or Head Start program, which are characterized by unfamiliar people, schedules, rules, and expectations, is not easy. Sharing, turn taking, planned napping, novel foods, toileting away from home, and self-care may be extremely demanding, resulting in a continuum of negative behaviors. Young children's reactions to this rite of passage depend on numerous factors. Past experience in child care or preschool may influence children's adjustment. They may have formed attachments and must begin anew. It is also possible that a child had social or learning difficulties previously and anticipates a negative experience in the new setting. A child who is distracted by family issues such as illness, divorce, or homelessness may also struggle when beginning school.

The fit between child and program is an important criterion in a child's acclimating to nursery or preschool. Some early childhood programs are overly academic or too rigorously structured for children, who may in turn act defiantly or even withdraw from interacting within the environment. Conversely, children who would thrive in a highly structured environment can become easily stimulated or overly aggressive in settings that provide too few boundaries or offer an excessive number of choices. Temperament—one's innate blueprint for behavior—may contribute to the ease with which a child feels comfortable away from home. Some children plunge right into new situations, exploring environments with enthusiasm and interest. Others may be slow to warm up and remain on the periphery, taking it all in while resisting any initial involvement with people or materials. Over time, with encouragement, their wariness may abate, and they may slowly begin to follow the daily routine. The patience and responsiveness of teachers or caregivers are critical here.

Kiani's behavior appears to be on the more challenging end of the behavioral spectrum. However, rather than their accentuating this negative aspect of her demeanor, it is critical for her teachers to step back and reframe their perceptions of Kiani in order to improve the overall tenor of her school experience. This takes tremendous effort and planning for teachers, as well as a psychic shift where they must make a conscious change in how they regard Kiani. By modifying their focus to Kiani's positive attributes, her teachers can see a child who has tremendous capabilities and potential. They will also see a child who has some social and emotional issues that need attention. Kiani's problems, while a part of her, do not define who she is. This approach is diametrically opposed to one in which her teachers direct their energies exclusively to getting Kiani to conform. In the latter, the teachers are more likely to fail.

Nonverbal Communication

As her teachers make efforts to acknowledge and build on Kiani's strengths, they are simultaneously more cognizant of their own nonverbal behaviors: frowns, sighs, and other signs of exasperation. Nonverbal communication is a powerful yet often unconscious response. A teacher's language, both verbal and nonverbal, is a strategic tool in modeling and supporting learning (Brady, Forton, Porter, & Wood, 2003). Kiani's teachers also need to self-reflect to ascertain if their verbal and nonverbal messages are congruent with how they are feeling. Children are quick to pick up inconsistencies in communications and may continue to maintain maladaptive patterns as a result (Seeman, 2000). Therefore, in practice, teachers need to come to terms with how they view a child and how they convey their feelings. In some cases, reconciling negative perceptions takes considerable work. It is reasonable for teachers to vent their feelings and frustrations and seek the advice of their colleagues. However, indiscriminate conversations in the presence of any child or adult is poor practice and harmful. Figure 5.1 shows the Teacher Self-Reflection Inventory (refer to Appendix D) as completed by one of Kiani's teachers to examine the teacher's own behavior.

Modifying the Learning Environment

Altering the learning and interpersonal environment for Kiani is essential. Tempering expectations for circle time is indicated here. If Kiani cannot make it through an entire activity (as is true of many children this age), then a shortened period would give her an opportunity for success. Starting with a short interval such as 3 to 5 minutes is a good beginning. Gradually increasing time within the group would help Kiani to realize that she is capable and is a part of the community. Assigning a helpful shadow or primary caregiver to quietly remind Kiani of the rules could be useful. A gentle hand on her shoulder or a whisper in her ear suggesting that she raise her hand might encourage Kiani to respond appropriately. Kiani might also benefit from one-on-one time with her teacher when she could receive undivided, positive attention. As demonstrated in the paradigm of "floor time," children benefit from having an adult be attuned to their specific needs and signals (Brazelton & Greenspan, 2000). In floor time, children are empowered to direct the play and interaction in a one-on-one situation. Having daily opportunities to assume a leadership role is a powerful gift. Allocating this time to slowly establish and practice communication could help Kiani gain a sense of control and lessen her tendency to melt down when stressed. Children spend much of their day being told what to do. Maintaining an overly rigid response and insisting on immediate compliance is not helpful in that it perpetuates a power struggle between a child and his or her teachers. At the same time, establishing a plan and maintaining consistency is critical for learning and incorporating the rules for the classroom.

As transitions are particularly problematic for Kiani, she personally needs advance warning before the change of activity takes place. Planned rehearsals of the transitions might also help Kiani know what to expect. Giving her a special object to take with her, in a modification of Winnicott's (1987) concept of the "transitional object," could allow Kiani to focus on something other than the change in activity and facilitate her getting from point A to point B. Providing Kiani with a task, such as carrying the purple ball, holding the door, or being the line leader, would also rechannel her energies in a more productive way.

Figure 5.1. Teacher Self-Reflection Inventory

Name <u>Beatrice</u>   **Date of Observation** <u>10/28/04</u>

Directions: Rate each item. Think about one or two examples to support each answer.

1 = never 2 = rarely 3 = sometimes 4 = often 5 = always

Tone

My tone is positive and nonthreatening.

    1   2   ③   4   5

I modulate my voice as a teaching tool.

    1   2   ③   4   5

My students understand my humor.

    1   ②   3   4   5

Comments

While I try to remain positive, Kiani's behavior really pushes my buttons. Lately, I notice that I focus on her negativity and am always reprimanding her.

Language

My students understand my vocabulary and the way I use language.

    1   2   3   ④   5

I state my expectations clearly.

    1   2   3   4   ⑤

I individualize my responses to each child.

    1   2   3   ④   5

Comments

What I do seems to work with most of the kids. But with Kiani, maybe I am not specific enough about my expectations during circle time or transitions. Just telling her to stop is not working.

Relationships with Children

I establish relationships with the children in my class.

    1   2   3   4   ⑤

I look at children's faces and body language to gauge their reactions.

    1   2   3   ④   5

I use active listening skills with the children.

    1   2   3   ④   5

Comments

I try to form a relationship with Kiani but am often put off. I wonder if she thinks that I don't really like her. She really tests me, and I find that irritating.

Classroom-Management Skills

I clarify classroom rules and expectations on a regular basis.

    1   2   3   4   ⑤

I respond consistently with logical consequences.

    1   2   ③   4   5

I encourage the children to communicate and problem solve.

    1   2   3   ④   5

Comments

I don't think I am consistent with Kiani, mostly because she is so difficult and I give up. While I think I am clarifying rules for the group, she obviously needs more individualized efforts in this area.

Reflections and Goals

It is hard to admit that having Kiani in my classroom is a tremendous challenge and that I am often grateful when she is absent. Maybe if I look at her strengths, I will like her more and she will respond by following the rules..

Negotiating is another method of assisting Kiani with her transition struggles. By offering a desirable activity at the end of the transition, Kiani may be inclined to shift gears more easily. For example, she might be promised special time with a book or the opportunity to set the table for snack if she leaves the gym without a fuss. The goal here would be to enable Kiani to be part of the solution, capitalizing on her leadership skills and perhaps minimizing her need to express herself through defiance. Another possible strategy might be the use of a sticker chart. Used consistently and defined clearly to the child, behavior charts are a concrete means of providing feedback to the child following the successful completion of an activity. Behavior modification, the use of rewards and punishments to shape behavior, should be implemented cautiously, as they can diminish a child's natural inclination or motivation to do the right thing (Kohn, 1999; Montessori, 1967). However, for some children an external incentive, whether in the form of praise or stickers, can mobilize a child in the short term. Teachers are advised to try alternatives before relying on compensation to change children's behavior. It is always necessary to review and modify behavior plans, as they tend to lose effectiveness over time. Distracting a child to avoid a conflict, such as letting him be the line leader, is a variation on behavior modification. Instead of rewarding desired behavior, an incentive is provided beforehand.

Because of Kiani's young age, a sticker chart would work best if it focused only on one venue and a limited number of behaviors (see Figure 5.2). Her teachers might choose to target circle time because it is a daily routine carried out at a set time and place. Kiani's "buy-in" to this process is imperative, so she should be allowed to choose the type and color of the stickers, in this case, pink smiley faces. Older children could also help participate in selecting the criteria and incentive.

Note that with a positive reinforcement plan, behaviors specified for reward are stated in the positive rather than negative (e.g., does not call out; does not shout). When Kiani has mastered the skills shown in Figure 5.2, more behaviors can be added, such as participation in group activities and responding to questions. Expectations can also be extended. At first, Kiani would get a sticker if she demonstrated the desired behavior once during circle time. With time, Kiani might need to exhibit the behavior consistently throughout the circle time to merit a reward. Eventually, Kiani would be expected to meet all three criteria before receiving a sticker. The ultimate goal is for Kiani to follow these classroom conventions without the need for external reinforcement. She would receive gratification from her teachers' smiles and praise and ideally from the activity itself. Other children might need a stronger incentive than just a sticker. Lunch with a teacher, extra computer time, or even a tangible prize could be given after

Figure 5.2. Kiani's Circle Time

	MONDAY	TUESDAY	WEDNESDAY	THURSDAY	FRIDAY
SITS WITH LEGS CROSSED		☺	☺	☺	☺
IS QUIET WHILE OTHERS TALK			☺		☺
RAISES HAND BEFORE SPEAKING					

the child reached a particular goal (e.g., demonstrating positive behavior five times within a week). The specific reward and time frame depends on what would motivate an individual child.

Communication with the Family

Another critical component in addressing Kiani's difficulties in school would be the involvement of her mother and grandmother. Building a trusting relationship with the family is critical here, as the teachers and caregivers need to work together to provide greater consistency for Kiani. The objective of discussions with Kiani's mother and grandmother would not be to place blame but rather to brainstorm on how best to understand and meet Kiani's needs. Using a communication journal that would go back and forth from home to school could help to facilitate the dialogue and better inform the teachers of Kiani's state when she arrives in school. Kiani could even be involved in the journal-writing process, by dictating how she is feeling at home or school. A small memo pad or notebook that can be put into a child's lunchbox or backpack is a convenient medium for communication. The following entries are taken from Kiani's journal:

> Nov. 3rd
> Overall, Kiani had a good day. She built a really tall tower of blocks with Ali and played nicely in the pretend play area with some of the other girls. Circle time is still a challenge for Kiani even though we've cut it down to 5 minutes for her. Since Kiani got soaked at the water table, she could use an extra change of clothes. Thanks.
> Beatrice

> 11/3
> I talked to Kiani about being bad during circle time and she promised to be good tomorrow. I'll send in a change of clothes.
> Mrs. Carter

> Nov. 4th
> Kiani tried very hard today during circle time. She even participated at one point. We're still working on sitting still and not calling out. Kiani seemed very sad today at naptime and kept saying that her mommy is coming to get her. Was she supposed to pick her up today?
> Beatrice

> 11/4
> Kiani's mother has not been home for a couple of days. I keep telling Kiani that she's coming back soon, I have no idea where my daughter is or when she's coming back. She does that from time to time. I know Kiani misses her mother.
> Mrs. Carter

> Nov. 5th
> Kiani was feeling a little sad today so she wanted to write to you. These are Kiani's words: "Grandma, I miss you. I want to go home. I miss Mommy. I'm being a good girl today."
> Beatrice

> 11/5
> Thank you for letting Kiani "write me" and tell me that she was a good girl in school. I tell her that school is very, very important. I took Kiani out to McDonald's for dinner as a special treat for being such a good girl.
> Mrs. Carter

This forum informed Kiani's teachers about the special circumstances at home that might have contributed to Kiani's mood as of late. It led to her teachers being extra sensitive to Kiani and gave her grandmother insight about her feelings while at school. Naturally, the willingness of teachers and parents to record their observations varies significantly. As demonstrated above, entries do not have to be lengthy, but they do need to be descriptive and clear.

Inviting Kiani's guardians to come into class to observe Kiani directly will further help them understand her issues. Reaching out to a social worker, school psychologist, or other administrators for additional input might be necessary to get support and to ensure a comprehensive perspective.

Occasionally, teachers in the same classroom disagree on how best to address behavioral problems. One teacher might be reluctant to approach a child, either because her style is more laid back or because she is unwilling or unable to physically intervene. Her colleague may perceive that response as either lazy or ineffective. Sometimes a teacher may respond by overindulging a child in order to prevent acting out. This response may be at odds with the teacher who wishes to set limits. These inconsistencies send a message to the child that she can play adults against one another. Resentment may build as one teacher feels the burden of responsibility to manage the misbehavior. Differences in disciplinary practice and role need to be aired in order to create a balance and some degree of consensus.

SELECTIVE MUTISM

Danielle is a 5-year-old attending full-day kindergarten. Since the beginning of the school year 6 months ago, she has refused to speak to any adults, though she selectively speaks with peers. Danielle readily engages in all group lessons and activities; however, she does so without verbalizing. Her classmates often ask why she does not talk to grownups, but Ms. Robinson avoids giving a direct answer. Recently, some of the girls in the class have become protective of Danielle and automatically speak for her. Danielle's parents know about her selective mutism, as it manifests itself with various family members, and have begun family therapy.

Danielle's behavioral difficulties in school are not overt. She is not disruptive or demanding, and she follows directions and complies with rules. Some teachers might even consider Danielle to be an ideal student. Yet Danielle's silence notably affects the social and emotional dynamics in her class. The other children observe her interactive style but cannot fully comprehend her complex psyche or motivations. Therefore, they are left to speculate on why a child who is capable of speaking would choose to remain silent. Some children

might see Danielle as a very powerful figure, one who exhibits tremendous control over her environment. It would not be unusual for some to emulate Danielle's behavior. Other children might be angry or frustrated by Danielle's apparent willfulness and make elaborate attempts to get her to speak, bringing excessive attention to the issue. As the preceding vignette suggests, some of Danielle's classmates have taken on a mothering role, believing they are helping by communicating for her.

Friendships

Establishing friendships, an important development for kindergarteners, consists of a beginning awareness and an understanding of others' perspectives (Elkind, 1994). Children of this age develop meaningful and satisfying relationships through play and verbal discourse, which includes sharing, listening, and responding appropriately (Thompson & Grace, 2001). Danielle's new friendships are atypical because of her intermittent verbal shutdowns. Her classmates do not understand her purposeful silences, causing some reluctance to interact with her. Without an adequate explanation from Danielle or Ms. Robinson, children may wonder or worry about what is wrong with Danielle. Even the girls who have chosen to align themselves with her may feel some ambivalence. While they want to be Danielle's friend, at times they may resent the undue responsibility they have assumed. Ms. Robinson might use a Peer Interaction Checklist (refer to Appendix C) to better illuminate the quality of her relationships (see Figure 5.3).

Theoretical Perspectives

The early childhood years between 3 and 5 are characterized by significant cognitive gains. Children are cognizant of physical and social relationships and continue their "meaning making endeavor" of the world (Piaget, 1954). They absorb facts and phenomena and offer insightful explanations for events they witness. In Piagetian theory, moving from preoperational thinking in which naive perceptions predominate to a more realistic and concrete representation of experiences involves active negotiations with others. Questioning about the practical and theoretical drives children's construction of knowledge during this

Figure 5.3. Peer Interaction Checklist

Name of Student <u>Danielle</u>   Grade/Class <u>K-3</u>

Date of Observation <u>2/9/04</u>   Observer <u>Mrs. Robinson</u>

Setting
- We've just finished circle, and the children have picked activities for center time. Danielle did not answer me when asked where she wanted to go. After the 21 other children in the class chose one of five stations, Danielle slowly walked over to the puzzle table and sat down. Three girls and a boy were already at the puzzle table.

Overall Behavior	Observed	Not Observed	N/A
Child typically engages in positive interactions with peers.	√		
Child has developed appropriate and meaningful relationships with peers.	√		
Child demonstrates tolerance when mildly provoked.			√

Comments

Overall, Danielle is a nice girl. The children like her, and the girls mostly include her, but at times they are frustrated and confused by her unwillingness to talk. Danielle sometimes hears the kids asking me why Danielle doesn't talk, and I don't really have a great answer for them. I just realized that Danielle prefers to hang out with girls because I rarely notice her in groups with boys. During this observation, Danielle worked on her puzzles (quietly) without speaking. I think this is because I was seated at the table. Is it also because Charlie was in the group?

Small Groups Within Classroom	Observed	Not Observed	N/A
Child expresses ideas clearly to peers.		√	
Child demonstrates ability to listen to peers.	?		
Child compromises as needed for the group process.		√	

Comments

Although, Danielle will speak to certain girls, I'm never able to hear the content of her verbalizations. As soon as I get close enough to hear, Danielle becomes quiet. I have no idea if Danielle listens to her friends. She sometimes looks at them while they speak, but not always. I do see her speaking after someone else has spoken, but I don't know if it is a direct response. If she doesn't answer the other children's questions, it would be understandable that they would find her odd.

Unstructured Periods (Lunch, Recess, Snack Time, Transitions)	Observed	Not Observed	N/A
Child finds a place within a group.	√		
Child refrains from following those who are misbehaving.			√
Child possesses ability to resolve conflicts peacefully.		√	

Comments

It's interesting that Danielle does not seem to have trouble during unstructured activities. Either she's invited to join a small group or she will quietly approach an individual or group. Danielle seems to be most comfortable with Heather and Britney, but there's no one she has conflicts with. I think that there will be increasing problems during the rest of the school year because some children seem to be losing patience with her.

period. Danielle is missing out on this essential cognitive growth experience because of the psychological conflict within her. If she were physically unable to speak, she would likely be taught sign language or a technological form of communication to allow her vital interactive opportuni-

ties. That is not a viable option for Danielle because her vocal apparatus is functional.

Another relevant construct for children 3–5 years of age is what Vygotsky (1978) referred to as the zone of proximal development. As explained in Chapter 1, the zone is attained when young children reach higher levels of cognition with the guidance of an adult or more competent peer. Vygotsky believed that interactions with peers and adults were an integral part of children's cognitive as well as social development. Through dialogue and play, the less accomplished child is encouraged to explore, test, and practice new skills and is helped to assimilate novel ideas. One can witness children achieving Vygotsky's conceptualization of the zone of proximal development by informally observing children at play. Danielle does not reach this zone with adults because she holds back sharing her opinions, predictions, and questions. Vygotsky would suggest that Danielle's full engagement in interactive experiences was necessary for optimal cognitive growth. While Danielle is learning passively, she is for the most part not an active participant in her education. Both Vygotsky and Piaget emphasized the need for a relationship between the learner and the environment in the acquisition of knowledge, concepts, and skills.

Understanding the necessity of Danielle's regaining her voice, the teacher worked closely with Danielle, her family, and her therapist. From ongoing communication with Danielle's parents, the teacher learned that Danielle willingly spoke on the telephone at home. As a creative solution, the teacher provided daily opportunities for Danielle to talk on a cell phone. Danielle was given one phone while her teacher spoke to her from another room using a second phone. Gradually, over the course of several months, the physical distance between Danielle and her teacher decreased. Eventually, Danielle would converse with her teacher by cell phone in the same room. By the end of the school year, Danielle felt comfortable enough to speak to her teacher without the aid of the telephone, and this milestone was generalized to other adults and children. Although there were occasional setbacks, the cell phones facilitated Danielle's breakthrough. This successful intervention was possible because of the support of the administration, who ensured that the class was covered when these telephone sessions took place. It was a superlative example of a school-based multidisciplinary individualized treatment plan (Dow, Sonies, Scheib, Moss, & Leonard, 1999), coordinating the efforts of the parents, teachers and clinicians.

Perhaps the greatest challenge for the teacher was addressing Danielle's special issues while simultaneously attending to the rest of the class. It is not unusual for children to have competing needs within a classroom community. Teachers naturally gravitate toward the child or children whose problems are the most glaring—the squeakiest wheel, so to speak. After all, teachers must prioritize. Fortunately for Danielle, she was noticed and undoubtedly benefited from her teacher's personalized attention. However, the teacher did not necessarily recognize the influence of Danielle's behavior on her classmates, who regarded her uniqueness with uncertainty and confusion. Some children inexplicably became her pseudoguardians, though they were not developmentally mature enough to effectively cope with this task. Children can adversely affect others in their surroundings when they perceive that their questions, concerns, and needs are secondary. However, children easily assimilate with a wide range of peers. Differences seem natural and are not necessarily obstacles to interaction. The key to creating harmony within a heterogeneous environment is ensuring that every child is observed and responded to in an individualized and sensitive manner.

OVERPROGRAMMING

Five-year-old Emma has an extremely busy life. Her after-school activities include Suzuki violin and ballet classes, swimming lessons, and gymnastics. Emma also has tutoring once a week to help her develop prereading skills and vocabulary. Additionally, she has frequent playdates, following her extracurricular classes. Emma comes to her kindergarten class dressed in the latest fashions and is averse to getting dirty. She complains about various aches and pains, is often reluctant to participate in activities, has frequent tantrums, and has on occasion been caught lying.

Emma presents a portrait of what David Elkind (2001) describes as a "hurried child." Elkind maintains that the consequences of our rapidly accelerating pace within society are higher expectations placed upon children. He bemoans the extinction of childhood, as we know it. The result is a highly pressurized growing-up experience with a demand for intellectual and social achievement. Parents are exposing their children to, if not bombarding them with, a myriad of activities and cognitive pursuits in an effort to "jump-start" their growth and development. Often, these children, reacting to undue stress and excessive overscheduling, act out in a variety of ways.

How can Emma's teachers understand the etiology of her aches, pains, and tantrums? Noting the quality of Emma's interactions with other children and adults as well as the time of day or activity that may trigger Emma's behaviors can yield some clues. As a first step in this inquiry, Emma's physical complaints need to be examined more thoroughly. A visit to the school nurse and an appointment with her pediatrician is indicated to rule out a physiological reason for her symptoms. Children who suffer from a cold or the flu or a chronic condition such as asthma may exhibit fatigue, clinginess, and tearfulness and, at times, misbehave to call attention to their discomfort. Certain medications also have behavioral side effects and must be considered when exploring the reasons for a child's behavior.

Emma may be reacting to the pressure of her overly demanding after-school schedule. Young children often express their worries through their bodies. According to a KidStress Survey, the three most frequent symptoms reported by children were insomnia, stomachaches, and just feeling sick (Witkin, 1999). Some examples of these "kid complaints" were "My stomach kills," "My stomach always hurts," or "I just ache all over." Behavioral symptoms such as temper tantrums were also reported in preschoolers who relied on physical instead of verbal coping mechanisms when stressed. Regression, moodiness, withdrawal, excessive clinginess, restlessness, and refusal to go to school may be additional behaviors exhibited by stressed-out children. Children need unhurried time in which to daydream and imagine, to process their day, and even to be bored. Emma's behavior may be a call for help—an admission that her day is too much for her and that she wants to slow down. Acting out through behavioral means or tantrums might be her nonverbal way of communicating her distress.

Emma's physical complaints may have another message as well. Perhaps she has a stomachache only when asked to perform a challenging activity in which she is afraid she will fail. It is possible

that her desire to excel causes her to withdraw rather than to persevere. Observing the specific circumstances under which Emma complains is important, to flush out this subtle communication. Modification of Emma's school day may involve additional downtime, quiet moments with the teacher, and reassurance that her work is valued unconditionally. Witkin (1999) cites school stress as children's greatest concern in their response to the KidStress survey. Older children worry about doing their work, getting good grades, meeting deadlines, and disappointing their parents. Getting ready in the morning, following new routines, and playing with other children can be extremely challenging for younger children. The daily ritual of saying good-bye can be painful, and the new faces of both children and teachers can be intimidating. Efforts on the part of the teachers to help Emma with this transition and to acknowledge her feelings might help her feel more comfortable in her kindergarten environment.

A meeting with Emma's parents can be extremely helpful in better understanding the underlying reasons for her behavior. Elkind (1988), in his examination of preschoolers at risk, looks at parenting practices as contributing factors. Emma's overscheduled day may be an effort on her parents' part to raise a "superkid," a practice that creates stress and, according to Elkind, is a form of miseducation. Some parents enroll their children in an excessive number of activities because they simply do not know how to keep them occupied. This tendency to overload may result in children being less able to entertain themselves. A discussion with Emma's parents about her needs, having realistic expectations for her, and the possible negative consequences of such a busy schedule might lead to some changes in her after-school calendar and, as a result, in her behavior. In preparation for a parent-teacher conference, Emma's teachers gathered the following anecdotes:

11/10/04
Emma was reluctant to participate during center time. She refused to choose an area, complaining that her stomach hurt. She sat quietly on a chair watching the children. When I asked her if she wanted to take a book, she said no, saying she was too tired. I asked her if she had gone to bed late

and she said no. I sent her to the nurse, but the nurse sent her back to class shortly after.

11/11/04

Emma came dressed to school in a lace dress and black patent leather shoes. When I asked her to come to the table to draw she said no and started to cry. When I approached her, she continued to protest, stating that she didn't want to get her dress dirty.

11/12/04

Emma was in the dramatic-play area with Megan and Shana. They were preparing dinner for their babies. Emma began protesting that the other two were taking the food that she wanted. I asked what was going on, and Megan and Shana said that Emma wasn't sharing. Emma immediately complained that her tummy hurt and left the area to sit by herself.

During a meeting with Emma's parents, her teachers will share these anecdotes to give them a more complete picture of what her day is like. The anecdotes should illustrate Emma's struggles without placing judgment or blame. Ideally, the teachers will not rush to provide solutions before the parents have a thorough understanding of what is going on in school. Giving their opinion too soon might put Emma's parents on the defensive. When Emma's parents ask what they could do to help Emma, the teachers could then seize the opportunity to share their perspectives. In discussing her after-school schedule, there would be a chance to see if that was beneficial for Emma. Her teachers might want to inform them that kindergarten is a place where it is acceptable to get dirty, and suggest that Emma's expensive clothing may inadvertently interfere with her willingness to participate. Educating Emma's parents about the typical activities that take place throughout the day may heighten their awareness of how Emma should come dressed to school. Ascertaining the role of dress in Emma's family would inform the teacher if Emma is worried that her clothing might get ruined and that her parents would be angry with her. Emma's worries could possibly contrib-

ute to her physical and behavioral symptoms, particularly if her parents caution her not to get dirty. Elkind (2001) warned parents and educators that dressing children as miniature adults with designer clothes can be harmful because it creates unrealistic expectations of the child.

Lying

Emma's teacher also has some concerns about Emma's not telling the truth. Children between 3 and 5 years of age do not have the same cognitive structures as adults and at times confuse reality and fantasy. Brazelton and Sparrow (2001) assert that lying is part of a 4-year-old mode of operation. Lying implies that children understand the difference between pretend and real, when in fact that is not always the case. An apparent lie may be an attempt to avoid being blamed or punished for misbehavior. Lying can also be a result of an intense wish for something. Through the untruth, a child may be more able to cope with the reality of not getting what he or she wants. If, for example, Emma said that her family got a puppy when it was known that she did not, the teacher might engage Emma in a conversation about how much she likes dogs and the different types of dogs that Emma knows. The use of diversion from the perceived fabrication helps both teacher and child to move forward. If the teacher confronted Emma about lying, Emma would likely stick to her story, and the two would be at an impasse. Labeling Emma's words as lies is not productive. It is best to avoid a confrontation and instead focus on the child's feelings or the desired behavior.

Emma's "lying" may also be related to her need to please and be accepted by her peers. Addressing her worries about being liked and having realistic expectations of herself may help Emma learn about the positives of being truthful. Learning to be honest is a long-term process that is acquired in part through the modeling of caring and accepting adults. Teachers can help in this journey by making it safe for children to tell the truth even when they are scared of the consequences. Circle time is an ideal venue for introducing the skill of role-playing. Here, the focus would be on the importance of telling the truth. The goal is for the children, Emma as well as her classmates, to relate the role-play to their own experiences. The following role-playing activity during circle time illustrates how early childhood teachers can address an issue without confrontation. This allows children to reflect without feeling threatened and being defensive.

Teacher: I'm going to pretend be a girl in our class who does not always tell the truth. She makes up stories to her friends and says that they are true. Christina has volunteered to play my friend in this role-play. Listen carefully because when we're done I'm going to ask you what you think.

Teacher: Hi Christina, guess what?

Christina: What?

Teacher: I'm going to be on television.

Christina: You are not. You're just a kid.

Teacher: I am too. And I'm going to make a lot of money, and buy a really big house and all the toys I want.

Christina: I don't believe you. You're lying.

Teacher: When I get my new house, you can come over and live in it too. And then we can be best friends, or even sisters.

Christina: You always make up stories. I don't want to be your friend.

Teacher: Please be my friend, Christina. I promise I won't make up stories anymore.

Following the dialogue, the teacher would ask her students to imagine how each child in the role-play feels. She would also ask them how they would feel if they were the children in the situation. They could speculate about why the child makes up stories and discuss how to be a good friend. This indirect method enables children to brainstorm and try out various solutions to problems. Note that effective role playing requires careful direction and practice.

Magical thinking (Brazelton & Sparrow, 2001; Fraiberg 1959), a variation on lying, is another characteristic of 4-year-olds. This may include imaginary friends who are sometimes conveniently blamed for infractions of the child. As with lying, teachers should avoid challenging the existence of pretend companions because it will only be met with resistance.

It should be noted that lying in older children needs to be considered differently. Children who can developmentally distinguish between reality and fantasy are cognizant of when they lie. Therefore, chronic lies in older children may be indicative of emotional or social concerns and need to be investigated further.

PRESCHOOL AGGRESSION

Three-year-old Ethan has recently begun attending nursery school 3 days a week, his first group experience. Ethan frequently grabs toys from other children and will sometimes hit to get what he wants. When his teacher tells him to stop, he will, but his grabbing and hitting subsequently resume. Some of the older children have verbalized their dislike of Ethan, while the younger ones exhibit fear of him. As a response to parents' complaints, the teacher is considering removing Ethan from the program.

Many young children go through periods when they exhibit behavior that is considered aggressive. Engaging positively with peers requires skills that many 3-year-olds have not yet mastered. Children do not fully understand the underlying causes of their emotions, and they cannot yet verbalize complicated or ambivalent feelings and wishes. They have less ability to control their actions, which are the result of frustration or worry that they do not comprehend. Sharing and waiting turns, behaviors necessary for group interactions, are not yet fully integrated into children's behavioral repertoire. Children learn normative behavior in part through ongoing experiences with peers that are guided by adults.

While aggressive behavior in 3-year-olds is not atypical, it can be vexing for teachers and caregivers who must protect all the children in their charge. Without adequate support, those children who do not seem to respond to discipline can overwhelm early childhood educators. They may doubt their abilities and wonder if they are cut out for their profession. Talking to colleagues who share similar experiences can provide early childhood educators with suggestions, alternative perspectives, and validation.

The Whole Child

If Ethan's teacher was introspective by nature or had collegial support, she might see beyond Ethan's aggressive behavior. She would not only think of Ethan as the kid who is hard to handle but also as the sweet child who requires special attention. Focusing on the positive in a child is not easy when a negative pattern dominates. However, when caregivers see a whole child—wit, intellect, preferences, and vulnerabilities—liking a difficult child is possible. Connecting on any level enables adults to be more tolerant and patient. The reasons for a child's poor social skills would then be carefully considered and solutions explored. Educators serve as positive role models; when they are more positive toward Ethan, the children will be as well.

Once Ethan's teacher has a broader view of him, one that includes his positive attributes, she may be more motivated to investigate the nature of his difficulties. She might discover that Ethan had few social experiences with peers prior to beginning nursery school and did not have sufficient opportunities to practice turn taking and using words to describe what he wants. If so, then Ethan would need time to internalize the rules for interaction and the consequences of not following the program's conventions. Social skills are not inborn and must be learned within a particular cultural venue.

Involving the Family

Communicating with Ethan's parents could also uncover clues about his struggles. The teacher might learn that Ethan's newborn sibling was taking up much of the family's time and energy and that there has been increased fighting with his 7-year-old brother. Ethan had become excessively whiney and clingy at home and expressed reluctance about leaving his mother to go to nursery school. This awareness would make Ethan's teacher much more sensitive to him. Children who want attention from adults will look for it in both positive and negative ways. If Ethan's teacher and parents together agreed to offer Ethan more special time, it might decrease his need to seek out negative attention. Reading books about new siblings and validating Ethan's ambivalent feelings about the new baby are tools for moving Ethan into a more socially positive mode.

A word of caution is warranted. While educators are encouraged to collaborate with families and look to them as the true experts on their children, teachers must delicately broach the subject of home issues. A teacher could unintentionally insult a parent or guardian simply by asking, "Is anything going on at home that I should know about?" Parents often feel that teachers blame them for faults in their children. They can be easily offended, especially when they already are concerned or feeling guilty. Teachers must first build a trusting relationship without judgment, so that parents feel safe to share their child-rearing problems. One possible way to successively involve parents would be to ask them to document their experiences, just as the teachers do at school. The Parent Observation Form (refer to Appendix F) encourages parents to be objective and focused. (If possible, the form would be translated into any non-English-speaking parents' native language.) It allows them to select those situations that tend to provoke troublesome behavior. The Parent Observation Form completed by Ethan's father is presented in Figure 5.4.

These brief comments from Ethan's father provide tremendous insight that can be used productively to help Ethan. From his father's observations, the teacher learns about the sibling dynamics and Ethan's neediness. This enriched understanding of Ethan's behavior will lead the teacher to be more attuned to him. She can also empathize with his parents' frustrations and gently guide them to anticipate Ethan's instigations, perhaps suggesting that Ethan may need their attention rather than the latest toy.

Involving Peers

As Ethan's teacher observes him and works collaboratively with his parents, she must also consider the feelings and behaviors of the other children in her care. They have shown their dislike for Ethan both verbally and nonverbally. While their attitude toward Ethan may be justified, it can inadvertently reinforce his negativity. The children in the class must learn techniques for coping with the situation. They need to be aware of when they can help Ethan and when they should leave him alone. By explaining to the children that Ethan is having a hard time but that he wants to be their friend, the teacher could build on their feelings of empathy and solicit their cooperation. Children are often the best teachers. Who better to show Ethan how to be a friend? Once the children are part of the process, they will be more apt to show compassion toward Ethan. Daily circle time is an opportunity for teachers to assist children in coping with complex and

Figure 5.4. Parent Observation Form

Date Feb. 8

Child's Name Ethan

Parent's Name Bradley Williams

Choose from the following situations that are problematic for your child. Complete one Parent Observation Form for each situation.

- Coming home from school
- Homework
- After-school activities
- Mealtime/food
- Playdates/peer interactions
- Waking up/Getting ready for school
- Traveling in the car
- Chores
- Following rules and routines
- Bedtime
- Grooming (baths, brushing teeth, toileting, dressing, etc.)
- Separations
- Sibling interactions
- Other

Problematic Situation Sibling Interactions

When It Occurs all the time—dinnertime, bedtime, weekends

Frequency/Duration until I threaten to take away their Game Boys and Game Cube

Observation Ethan is always bothering his brother Jared. Jared is 7 and doesn't always want to play with his little brother. Ethan goes into Jared's room and takes his toys without asking. Somehow the toys usually end up broken. Then all hell breaks loose.

Your response I get really angry with Ethan, because he has to learn to respect his brother's property. I work very hard and don't want to deal with this when I come home. My wife has given up because she says they fight all day long and she's busy with the baby. Taking away their video games is the only thing that works.

What do you think is really going on? I guess he's looking for attention. We give him a lot of stuff—all the newest toys—but it's never enough. I guess he could use some friends of his own, that's why we put him in nursery school. But that's not working out.

challenging peer interactions. Role-playing within that circle helps young children develop communication skills that can be useful with a range of peers and situations. Dramatic-play experiences can also promote social competence in children with varied temperaments and abilities.

DYSFUNCTIONAL FAMILIES

Aiden's behavior has deteriorated significantly throughout his kindergarten year in a parochial school. His parents are in the process of a divorce, and Aiden is regularly exposed to his parents' show of animosity toward each other. In class, Aiden has a low frustration threshold and can be defiant, especially when confronted with reactions to his misbehavior. His physical outbursts include kicking, hitting, head butting, biting, and spitting. Aiden uses a plethora of expletives when he is upset. Most distressing to his teachers is Aiden's intense crying in response to being removed from an activity or the classroom. Despite his behavior, Aiden is a popular boy.

Divorce, even under the most amicable circumstances, can provoke a range of behaviors in children of all ages that are uncharacteristic of them. Given that one out of two American marriages ends in divorce (Gestwicki, 2000), educators must be prepared to support children and their families through this difficult time, which may last as long as a few years. The effects of divorce may be short term or longer lasting, depending on the age of the particular child and his or her resilience and coping skills. The way in which the parents deal with the emotional consequences of the separation, the degree to which the split influences the child's day-to-day routines, as well as the nature of available support also have an impact. Because these factors can vary even within a family, it is possible for one sibling to be more significantly affected. It is also feasible that a child will not manifest any noticeable symptoms, yet it is imperative that adults vigilantly watch for signs of stress over time. Schools cannot avoid getting involved when the effects on the child are profound and the parents regularly share their concerns with the educators.

Children will respond to an impending or finalized divorce in a multiplicity of ways. Difficulty sleeping, eating, concentrating, and regression to earlier stages of development are frequently observed. Increased anger and frustration are also common, as young children may not be able to pinpoint and articulate the source of their unhappiness. Some children are reluctant to discuss the change in their family structure because they are embarrassed, have not yet accepted the inevitable, or are not developmentally mature enough to understand such a complex situation. Older children, in particular, do not want to stand out from their peers and may be reticent about discussing what is going on at home. Others are extremely verbal about their feelings and readily convey their experiences, sometimes to the point of irritating peers.

In divorce, children must adapt to new living arrangements that may also be accompanied by a change in financial status. It is not unusual for mothers to return to full-time work following a divorce to make ends meet. While this can be a positive experience for a mother who is creating a new life for herself, it can also be seen as another loss to a child who previously had his or her mother available all the time. Moving to a new home can also contribute to feelings of uncertainty and anxiety. Regardless of the family finances, children's heightened need for time and attention during this critical period must be paramount.

Teachers who are assisting a child through a troubling divorce may feel that there are competitive forces at play. Despite parents' genuine caring and concern for their children, the pain of divorce sometimes makes them self-involved, often at the expense of their children. Children often find themselves in the middle of a power struggle between their parents. Teachers who have unlimited understanding for the egocentricity exhibited by young children may not be as patient with adults. Yet being receptive to a parent who is hurting and who has few or no family and friends is good practice. Remaining compassionate while not being pulled into an unwanted role of psychologist or friend takes skill and tact. Teachers need to set boundaries while gently reminding parents to refocus their attention on their child or seek professional counseling for themselves and their child.

Staying neutral can be difficult for teachers when it seems that one parent was wronged by the other. However, appearances can be deceiving and teachers are advised to not take sides. This can be fairly tricky during parent-teacher conferences when one parent manipulates the teacher to argue his or her point in a heated debate. Heads-up planning can prevent a teacher from becoming trapped in such an uncomfortable predicament. Sometimes the issue at hand is whether a child should continue to attend a religious or private school. Teachers can inadvertently give credence to one parent's claim if they are not cautious. With some ex-couples, being in the same room together inevitably leads to confrontation, and separate parent-teacher conferences should be scheduled. Here, teachers must be diligent about sharing the same observations, concerns, and requests at both conferences. Arranging duplicate copies of report cards, invitations to school events, and perhaps school work is a time-consuming task that must be carried out consistently. Schools should keep copies of custody agreements on file to guarantee that their obligations are fulfilled.

Without specific training in this area, early childhood and elementary school educators must extend their role and provide emotional and psychological support to children. Because preoperational children view events in their world as emanating from their own needs (Piaget, 1926), children often shoulder the blame for their parents' separation. Over time, these children need to be reassured that they are not responsible. Children may also need to be dissuaded from trying to get their parents to reconcile.

Aiden's response to his parents' divorce may be extreme, but it is not unique. His emotions are tumultuous and include anger, frustration, resentment, fear, guilt, and worry. These feelings are powerful and overwhelming. His needs are no longer the focal point in his family, and Aiden is spiraling downward. Aiden's family requires professional intervention, and his teachers have a responsibility to help them secure the appropriate services. To that end, teachers must document their observations of Aiden, share their experiences, and make a firm request for therapy (e.g., play therapy or art therapy) perhaps more than once. Some parents do not immediately follow through on suggestions made by their child's teachers or administrators. Often, parents need time to process what has happened to their family and may not be ready to accept what their child needs. It is advantageous for the school to provide a list of qualified psychotherapists who accept the family's health insurance plan. When the family has no insurance, the local mental health association can locate practitioners who base their fee on a sliding scale. Once Aiden begins to receive psychological support, the school's administrators should request permission for the teacher to speak to his therapist. Ideally, the therapist would be invited to observe Aiden within the classroom setting to facilitate an interdisciplinary team approach between administration, teachers, therapist, and parents. A support group for children of divorce led by the school's psychologist or social worker is also indicated.

In school, Aiden's teachers struggle to maintain a peaceful environment when his behavior is particularly disruptive. Aiden's issues sometimes overshadow the activities and accomplishments of the other children. To manage Aiden when he decompensates, the principal had been removing him from the classroom. This was done in part to protect the other children but also as a punishment. Wanting Aiden to be fully integrated into the classroom, his teachers decide to stop routinely calling the principal for help. They want Aiden to see them as willing and able to help him. The teachers are guiding Aiden to be more cognizant of his own emotions and to connect them to the way he behaves. They developed a private signal that Aiden can use when he feels he is losing control and needs the teachers' attention or to be away from the other children. One-on-one time with a teacher gives him an opportunity to calm down. This dynamic is restorative, as it allows him to learn coping skills and to regain control while preserving his dignity within the classroom. There is also a quiet, private space within the classroom that is available to the children when they need alone time.

Aiden's teachers have opted to ignore his unsuitable language for now in the hope that the cursing will lose its power when not reinforced with attention. When young children first use curse words, it is usually because they are mimicking what they hear, in some cases on school buses. They soon discover that adults and older children respond rather strongly and that these are special words. Some children purposefully verbalize inappropriately to get a desired response from adults. Aiden's teachers notice that he only curses when he is angry. Correcting Aiden does little to change the situation because he cannot respond reasonably when he is enraged. Selective ignoring and removal of the anticipated shock factor is often sufficient to extinguish the undesirable behavior.

HEART START PRINCIPLES

The practicing, communicating, learning, and testing of boundaries that take place during the preschool and kindergarten years set the stage for the ongoing educational world into which the young child is about to embark. This growth and development occur not only in the cognitive sphere, but in the social-emotional realm as well. Griffin (1994) highlights the importance of the emotional foundations of school readiness that go beyond the stereotypical three Rs. Heart Start, a language of school readiness, refers to social-emotional skills as prerequisites to successful learning. This framework includes seven characteristics that are the foundation for later learning.

1. *Confidence:* A sense of control and mastery of one's body, behavior, and world. The child's sense that he is more likely than not to succeed at what he undertakes, and that adults will be helpful.
2. *Curiosity:* The sense that finding out about things is positive and leads to pleasure.
3. *Intentionality:* The wish and capacity to have an impact, and to act upon that with persistence. This is clearly related to a sense of competence, of being effective.
4. *Self-Control:* The ability to modulate and control one's own actions in age-appropriate ways; a sense of inner control.
5. *Relatedness:* The ability engage with others based on the sense of being understood by and understanding others.
6. *Capacity to communicate:* The wish and ability to exchange ideas, feelings, and concepts with others. This is related to a sense of trust in others and of pleasure in engaging with others, including adults.
7. *Cooperativeness:* The ability to balance one's own needs with those of others in a group activity. (p. 6)

All these characteristics are essential for the young learner to adapt to school and be able to absorb the richness of the cognitive, social, and emotional environment. However, with a current emphasis in schools on test scores that merely reflect a child's academic prowess, it is rare that curriculum prioritizes the acquisition of these vital skills. As a result, some children are moving on from pre-K and kindergarten lacking qualities that will promote their learning. The pressure from high-stakes testing puts further stress on children who are already vulnerable in the social-emotional sphere, possibly contributing to an increase in behavioral difficulties in the classroom. It is hard for public school teachers to balance curricular mandates and at the same time provide an environment that adequately prepares children for lifelong learning. Some states, including New York and New Jersey, require character education as part of their standards to facilitate the development of social skills. However, the methods by which this is fulfilled vary considerably from district to district. To be successful, social skills programs need to be integrated, reinforced, and generalized throughout the school day during group, individual, and center time. Without consistent and thoughtful attention to education that stresses social skills and emotional intelligence (Goleman, 1995), children will not be equipped to handle the rigor of more sophisticated interpersonal classroom challenges as they get older. The ensuing behavioral consequences disrupt learning on both the individual and group level.

CONCLUSION

Developmental discipline, coupled with a comprehensive social skills curriculum, targets challenging behaviors from early on to ensure an optimal educational experience. With both teachers and families sharing their observations and collaborating on problem solving, children are more successful. Building on this chapter, we recommend that teachers do the following:

- Anticipate that children need time to adjust to separations
- Avoid labeling children's differences as behavior problems
- Look for positive attributes in children
- Pay attention to children's nonverbal communication
- Recognize the importance of peer interactions and friendships
- Use behavior modification strategies sparingly, and always customize them to the particular child
- Invite parents to engage in formal observations of their children

CHAPTER 6

School-Ager Issues

Eight-year-old Nicholas repeatedly comes to school without his homework. Mrs. Conner, his teacher, has observed that Nicholas copies the assignment from the board but rarely completes or turns in all the required homework. When Mrs. Conner asks about it, he responds with a shrug and does not give a definitive answer when pressed about the issue. Nicholas states that his mother does not care whether he does his assignments or not, believing that it is only busy work. In conversations with Nicholas's mother, Mrs. Conner learns that she is a single parent who is not home when he returns from school. Both the babysitter and Nicholas's mother engage in daily homework battles with him. His mother attributes his resistance to the fact that he has Attention Deficit Hyperactivity Disorder (ADHD).

HOMEWORK BATTLES

Nightly struggles over homework are common. Children approach the task in various ways depending on their temperament, learning styles, interest level, motivation, and abilities. Some rush through their assignments, with sloppy, incomplete results. They may wait until the last minute for long-term projects, asking to go to the library the night before the assignment is due. Others are so meticulous about their final product that they perseverate over details, and the completed work takes an inordinate amount of time. After-school activities sometimes interfere with homework if parents do not convey that it is a priority. "IMing" friends, checking baseball scores, playing video games, and watching television are other distractions that compete for children's attention. As a result, homework is sometimes begun too late in the evening, when children are already fatigued. Homes can also be too noisy and chaotic for children to concentrate. For some children, homework is just too hard to do without adult support. Their parents might be too busy or not present at all, and subsequently homework does not get done. On the other side of the continuum are parents who may think they are helping by actually doing the work rather than guiding their child through the process.

There are several reasons why Nicholas may not be prepared for school. Lacking adequate help, he has grown accustomed to getting away with not doing his homework. He may be telling his mother he has completed his assignments when he has not, and she does not have the strength to follow through with him. Given his difficulties concentrating on a task for an extended period of time, he may have reached his satiation point by the time school is over. His medication for ADHD might wear off by late afternoon, which compromises his attention span. He also could have learning disabilities that interfere with his ability to organize and process information. There may additionally be gaps in Nicolas's knowledge base because of his tendency to tune out.

Although Mrs. Conner knows that Nicholas copies his assignments from the board, it is unclear if he omits vital information. Perhaps the directions are vague, and he does not know how to begin. Rather than ask for clarification or do his work incorrectly, Nicholas might prefer to avoid it altogether. Questioning the teacher, particularly if he is worried about seeming stupid, is not easy. Time constraints during the school day could prevent Mrs. Conner from being available for explanations. It is also possible that the actual assignments are uninteresting, even unreasonable, and not developmentally or academically appropriate. The material may not have been taught effectively, and as a result, Nicholas gives up rather than attempt something he does not understand. His mother, already overwhelmed by having sole responsibility for his care, may not have the skills to assist him. She might be unfamiliar with the material itself or have learned it through different methods. As a result, she may yield to his resistance rather than work with him to help him overcome his weaknesses. Nicholas is spiraling into a pattern that is neither productive nor conducive to his academic success.

Supporting Families

A proper setting is critical for children to learn the importance of their homework. Parents need to establish this environment early on in their children's educational lives. A space that is clutter free, separated from distractions such as television, video games, and extraneous conversations is essential. Providing such necessary materials as sufficient paper, writing implements, and a dictionary also helps children complete their work. A checklist, for example, the one shown in Figure 6.1, can be distributed to parents at the beginning of the school year to serve as a reminder of the necessary ingredients for homework success.

Depending on a particular child's temperament, activity level, and distractibility, a specific time frame may be designated for homework completion. Some children prefer to tackle their assignments as soon as they return home from school, while others need some downtime or a snack, to help them refuel after a long day. Children, who procrastinate past the dinner hour with requests for "just one more show" lack the cognitive energy necessary for fulfilling their responsibilities.

Young children such as Nicholas might benefit from doing their work in the kitchen or in a com-

Figure 6.1. Homework Environment Checklist

Suitable lighting
☐ Natural light if possible

Minimal noise in room
☐ Soft instrumental music is acceptable

Limited distractions
☐ No television, radio, video games
☐ No unrelated conversations in room

Sufficient space for work materials (varies with task)
☐ Clutter free

Good writing surface
☐ Desk or table
  or
☐ Clipboard/slant board

Proper seating
☐ Non-swivel chair that is size appropriate (feet reach floor and back is supported)
  or
☐ Cushion to support back if seated on floor, bed, or couch

Materials that may be needed for assignments are easily accessible
☐ Paper (lined, construction, graph, scrap, index cards, stick-on notes)
☐ Pencils/pens/markers/crayons/highlighters
☐ Erasers/correction fluid/pencil sharpener
☐ Scissors/glue/paper clips/stapler
☐ Ruler/protractor/compass/calculator
☐ Folders
☐ Dictionary/thesaurus
☐ Word processor/Internet

munal space under a parent or caregiver's watchful eye. Questions may need to be answered and the acquisition of new learning skills guided, encouraged, and reinforced. While it is not always realistic for parents or guardians to be present to supervise homework, children's work should be reviewed until the children are sufficiently independent. Homework is not expected to be mistake free. Teachers use homework to assess what areas are problematic for their students and to then review as indicated. When there is a major discrepancy between the quality of schoolwork and homework, teachers know that parents are more involved than they should be. Communication between teachers and parents can clarify expectations about how parents should support their children's learning.

The impact of Nicholas's home learning environment as well as his attention deficits should be explored. Both Mrs. Conner and Nicholas's mother can work together to better structure homework time, beginning with a closer look at his strengths, weaknesses, and interests. Perhaps Nicholas's work needs to be modified—quantitatively, qualitatively, or both. Tempering requirements to be more reasonable given his short attention span may be helpful.

Homework Guidelines

At the beginning of the school year, teachers must establish homework guidelines and state their expectations regarding parental involvement. This information needs to be reviewed and reinforced over the course of the year. When communicating with families, educators must take into account children's varied backgrounds and languages. All letters and notices must be written in straightforward language to ensure mutual understanding of the child and parent's role. Translation into additional languages may also be necessary, depending on the population served.

Teachers can offer strategies for those children who struggle with homework completion. For example, a timer can be useful for children who take too long to finish their work, as well as for those who have trouble sitting for prolonged periods of time. This needs to be determined on an individual basis between teacher and parent. For the younger child, or for the child who is disorganized, the teacher must make sure the homework is copied thoroughly into a planner or notebook and that the necessary materials are placed in the child's backpack. To save time and avoid distress, some teachers opt to have prepared copies of the homework assignment for children who find writing or copying particularly arduous. Part of the child's homework may include a parent's signature indicating that the work has been checked. The overall goal would be to wean children away from these steps once they are able to take responsibility for their own work. Mastery of these skills can take quite some time.

A child's attitude and approach to homework are important emotional indicators for the teacher.

The developmental discipline method encourages teachers to consider the whole child. Information that is gleaned during observations is useful in developing individual strategies that will minimize homework struggles. Parents need to communicate with their child's teacher if the work is too difficult or takes an excessive amount of time. Teachers rely on feedback from parents to help them judge whether their assignments are realistic. For a child with special needs, trouble with homework may necessitate a reassessment of goals by the child-study team. Together with the parent and teacher, new, more targeted goals may be instituted for the short term to enable the child to overcome his or her homework challenges.

ATYPICAL SOCIAL SKILLS

Since kindergarten, Ashley has had trouble getting along with peers. Now a third grader, she is regularly antagonistic, defiant, and both verbally and physically hurtful toward her classmates. Few girls in the grade are willing to include her in their free-time activities, and Ashley frequently complains that everyone is being mean to her. Boys and girls are quick to blame Ashley for problems, and unsupervised interactions between Ashley and her classmates typically lead to arguments. Some parents have told their children to stay away from Ashley. Ashley says that she does not want or need friends. Her teacher, Miss Romano, is frustrated, because she is not able to provide Ashley with the constant assistance Ashley needs in social situations. Miss Romano worries that Ashley will never be able to repair the harm she has done to other children and consequently to herself in this school.

Ashley's ongoing problems with peers may seem insurmountable. Miss Romano has attempted to help Ashley engage positively, but has not been effective for any length of time because the children seem fixated on past altercations. A history of dislike and mistrust between Ashley and her classmates keeps Ashley from moving forward. Whether in working groups or recess, Ashley's feelings of being wronged and her classmates' unwillingness to give her another chance inevitably lead to conflict.

Miss Romano has a huge task ahead because she must not only address the social climate in her class but must also explore the contributing factors over the past 4 years:

- How have Ashley's difficulties been addressed in earlier grades?
- What are the contexts in which Ashley interacts cooperatively?
- Are the feelings and behaviors of Ashley's peers being considered?
- Have Ashley's parents been enlisted?
- Is Miss Romano fully aware of the complexity of the social dynamic within her class, or does she focus exclusively on Ashley?

Connectedness, or a sense of belonging, is a human need (Maslow, 1954). People typically seek out others for comfort and companionship, although they differ in their preference for solitude. Most children enjoy satisfying peer relationships beginning in infancy or toddlerhood (Thompson & Grace, 2001). They develop interpersonal skills, among them speaking, listening, turn taking, and cooperation, gradually and steadily over time. Struggles and conflicts result as children practice and test these abilities. Learning ensues as past encounters bring new awareness and expertise to future social interactions. With minimal adult intervention, children gravitate toward peers and take pleasure in talking, working, and playing. By 9 years of age, it is common for children to have at least a couple of close friends and to also be part of a larger clique of the same gender (Wood, 1997).

For a small number of children, learning to engage with friends is not a natural process. Because of innate temperament and environmental experiences, some children do not easily assimilate conventional social skills. Systematic instruction and supervised facilitation is thereby required. Children also benefit from psychotherapy to reveal underlying or overt anger, depression, or anxiety.

Ashley's difficulties seemingly went unchecked for so long that it ultimately poisoned an otherwise normal social setting. Children who had previously included Ashley in their play despite her actions

towards them reached their tolerance threshold. Ashley's predicament may be even more distressing because she is a girl; some 8- and 9-year-old girls may be less forgiving and hold on to grudges longer than boys. Boys who are not so dependent upon verbal exchanges can work out their differences physically on an athletic field. Ashley was not welcomed back into the fold even when there were reprieves for her unkind behavior.

Adaptations in School

Helping Ashley necessitates radical modifications to her school routine: removing her from social situations where she is bound to fail. The three most problematic areas are sitting in clusters with other children in the classroom, eating in the lunchroom, and participating in unstructured recess. Hinson (2001) highlights the many problems that arise in typical, unstructured recess. He suggests that children who are overactive become even more hyper in the absence of formalized activities. Simultaneously, there are children like Ashley who cannot socialize without guidance. These children are unable to engage positively with others and use recess time productively. Without carefully orchestrated games, Ashley acts out in order to connect on some level to the group. While restructuring recess might be advantageous for Ashley and others who struggle during this time, another option is to provide her individual attention away from the tumult of the large group.

Supervising Ashley apart from the other children is a major undertaking and requires commitment on the part of the faculty, but it is crucial in undoing ingrained, predictable responses. Ashley's teacher, and ideally an administrator, would alternate lunching with Ashley. Not a punishment, this special lunchtime would allow Ashley to express her feelings, attain undivided positive attention, and direct the interactions (see discussion of floor time in Chapter 5). For example, books could be read, games played, or research conducted on the computer. Keeping in mind Ashley's weaknesses, the teacher or administrator should eventually encourage Ashley to invite a friend to join them. In incremental steps, the number of children participating would increase (to a maximum of four or five) and the amount of adult facilitation and mediation decrease. The following anecdotes by

Miss Romano illustrate the progression from Ashley's individualized lunchtime to successful small groups.

October 2003

Ashley was initially angry when I told her that she would be having lunch and recess with me every day. She said it wasn't fair that only she got into trouble because the other kids are so mean to her. I emphasized that this was not a punishment but rather a way for her to have an enjoyable break time. When asked, she said that she would want other kids to join us but couldn't name anyone that she liked. Ashley is clearly lonely, and I don't want to further isolate her, but I know leaving her to fend for herself in a large group just doesn't work. I'm hoping some one-on-one time with me will build her confidence and get her to think a little bit before acting.

November 2003

Our daily lunch and recess have turned out to be very pleasant for Ashley and for me. She's a talented girl who sings, dances, and designs clothes. Her mood has improved a bit over the last couple of weeks, and she seems to relish our special time together. Today, Ashley invited Sarah to join us. At first Sarah was not thrilled, but she ended up having a good time. I let the girls play on my computer. Ashley was reluctant to let Sarah have a turn so I had to intervene. After Ashley saw that Sarah was being particularly nice to her, Ashley offered Sarah half of her doughnut. Small steps . . . Ashley asked Sarah to come back tomorrow and Sarah said yes.

December 2003

Today's lunch and recess was very challenging. Ashley invited Sarah and Elizabeth. Elizabeth and Sarah are best friends. I had a feeling this might not work, but it's what she wanted, and the two girls were willing to come. Ashley

very much wants to be their friend, but she inevitably ends up antagonizing them. Every time Sarah and Elizabeth spoke to each other, Ashley tried to physically place herself between them. I tried to distract them from the tension in the room by initiating conversation and suggesting games. While Sarah and Elizabeth were enthusiastic, Ashley vetoed every suggestion. She complained that the girls were excluding her, but she made no attempt to cooperate.

January 2004

Some days are better than others with Ashley. I've discovered that when I choose the children who join us for lunch and recess, and I determine the activities, she will more likely participate pleasantly. However, when I give Ashley too much freedom, it tends to go awry. Having boys in the group does not seem to make any difference. With structure and supervision, Ashley can be a fun and cooperative playmate. Fortunately, the children in our class are getting to see this positive side, and our enjoyable interactions have carried over into the classroom, though inconsistently.

The goal of these private recess/lunchtimes is for Ashley to return to her regular routine. However, it could be a considerable length of time before Ashley is ready for this monumental step. An adult specifically assigned to keep an eye on Ashley would help ensure a successful transition back into the large group.

At the same time that Ashley was receiving individualized support, the rest of the third graders would be learning self-reflection and coping strategies to aid them in relating positively with Ashley. This is best achieved with ongoing class meetings, possibly combined with a predesigned social skills program (see Chapter 2). Through structured discussions and role-playing, students would think about their own behavior and discover productive solutions to interpersonal problems. Rules of engagement must be clearly determined to prevent the process from becoming a destructive forum in which classmates are named and blamed. Ashley might feel that her classmates were ganging up on her if she was the focus of the sessions. Yet if the group refrained from pinpointing individuals and was both nonjudgmental and supportive in nature, Ashley might be willing to describe her own perceptions. The door would be open for genuine dialogue and problem solving. Children would learn to recognize other viewpoints and work toward common goals. One resolution could be in the form of a "peace treaty," a signed document pledging to be respectful and inclusive to all classmates. Peer pressure can be a powerful motivator or impetus for change in school. Here, peer pressure would be orchestrated for the betterment of the community.

Reaching Out to Families and Professionals

Working with Ashley's parents is clearly pivotal for her development. They can provide information about Ashley's functioning outside of school, support the school's efforts, and make suggestions based on what they have observed to be effective. The faculty can reassure Ashley's parents that their child is genuinely cared for and that structures are in place to help her succeed. They would likely make a recommendation that Ashley receive professional services in the form of individual therapy and a social skills group. If Ashley's parents were resistant to the idea of psychological assistance, the school would be instrumental in helping them recognize it is what Ashley needs. With diligence and persistence the educational team would hopefully persuade Ashley's parents to attain services for her.

There are those who would argue that schools are not responsible for children's psychological well-being. After all, teachers are not trained to be psychologists or social workers and may not always know how to advise families about psychological evaluations, counseling, and alternative therapeutic schools/settings. When a child does not follow a typical pattern of development (Elkind, 1994; Wood, 1997), educators must carefully document observations. These observations may later be used when providing evidence that professional assistance is warranted. A list of red-flag behaviors (see Figure 4.2) can further alert teachers and administrators if outside consultation is necessary. Observing a behavior on this list

does not in itself indicate that there is a problem. However, noting a constellation of behaviors over time may suggestion a need for intervention. Given the overcrowding and teacher shortages in many public schools, there is not enough people power to fix all the problems concerning children and their families. That said, teachers cannot successfully educate students if the students are not emotionally available for learning. For teachers to do their job well, they must see their responsibilities as being comprehensive and be available to children and their families.

ANXIETY AND DEPRESSION IN CHILDREN

Hailey has always been a quiet and reserved child. This year as a second grader, she has withdrawn from both children and adults. Often teary, Hailey seems sad and tense. Hailey excels academically but is averse to participating in group discussions. She recently started refusing to eat in the lunchroom and spends lunchtime and recess with her teacher or an administrator or in the main office. Her parents have informed the principal that they are concerned because Hailey says that she doesn't want to go to school anymore. Mornings are very difficult for everyone when Hailey will not enter the school building after being brought by her mother.

Hailey presents with three specific behavioral issues: her reluctance to enter school, to go to the lunchroom, and to communicate with peers. Coupled with her apparently fragile emotional state, Hailey is a child in crisis. It would be reasonable to direct the intervention primarily to her noncompliance, especially because her actions are a burden to the school's staff. However, that would not address the core of Hailey's difficulties or the cause of her regressive behavior. Attempts to modify her behavior without attending to her thoughts and feelings would not result in permanent change, and the problem could possibly manifest itself in another form. Hailey must be assessed holistically (physically, emotionally, socially, and cognitively) with consideration given to the interaction between these systems.

Hailey's problem is complex and may emanate from more than one source. A combination of factors is often responsible for behavior patterns. Discerning all the possible reasons for Hailey's escalating isolation and then zeroing in on the operating variables take time and teamwork. Hailey's parents initiated the process by sharing their concerns, and now the school should follow up with a meeting. Those who work closely with Hailey—the classroom teacher, the principal, and perhaps a specialist—would come to the meeting with documented observations of Hailey in various contexts of the school day. The goal of this first meeting would be to better understand the nature of Hailey's distress and determine the direction for intervention or further investigation.

Brainstorming with Hailey's parents would hopefully yield pertinent information about her underlying issues. They would describe her early development and prior group experiences and draw possible links to her current situation. Her parents could note if Hailey was similarly troubled outside school and whether the problem suddenly appeared or was progressive. Sometimes children are afraid to leave home, not because of school, but because of worries at home. Hailey had already confided in her parents about her feelings regarding school so they could probe for further details. Is she being teased or bullied? Did she witness or experience a traumatic event? Does Hailey have concerns about her academic achievement or about her relationship with her teacher?

Along with the family's invaluable insights, the faculty would interject their own anecdotes related to Hailey's affect and interpersonal interactions. An innocuous vignette where a child jokingly called Hailey weird could turn out to be significant. The discussion should also explore Hailey's reluctance to raise her hand in class; participate in class discussions; and go to large, noisy venues such as the lunchroom. Hailey's teachers would suggest that she displays heightened anxiety and depression in academic and social situations and needs professional help. A medical and possible neurological examination is called for to establish if she would benefit from therapy, medication, or both. This outside intervention would be in conjunction with a plan for alleviating Hailey's stress while she is in school and, if indicated, at home as well.

Background Information

Anxiety and depression in children is not a new phenomenon. By the end of the 19th century, the field of childhood psychopathology was clearly established and there was great interest in children's psychological health (Knopf, 1984). At that time, the child-study movement's systematic approach to observing children's behavior and, later, Freud's psychoanalytical theory focused on the frustrations and emotional conflicts of childhood. The fourth edition of the *Diagnostic and Statistical Manual of Mental Disorders* (American Psychiatric Association, 1994) defines several forms of childhood anxiety, including separation anxiety disorder, generalized anxiety disorder, overanxious disorder of childhood, and posttraumatic stress disorder. Anxiety and depression can overlap with obsessive-compulsive disorder, panic attacks, social phobia, selective mutism, and trichotillomania. When left untreated, these maladies can lead to social isolation, peer rejection, loneliness, and low self-esteem.

Currently, the prevalence of anxiety and depression in school-aged children is staggering. Research on children 9 to 17 years of age indicates that levels of anxiety, which are strongly linked to depression, increased substantially from the 1950s to the 1990s (Twenge, 2000). Twenge noted that contemporary "normal" children report the same level of anxiety and depression as children in the 1950s who were psychiatric patients. Anxiety disorders are said to afflict 12–20% of children and adolescents in the United States (Velting, Setzer, & Albano, 2002). In particular, anxiety-based school refusal is said to affect 2–5% of school-aged children (Anxiety Disorder Association of America, 2003). Recent studies also show that up to 2.5% of elementary school children experience a clinically significant episode of depression (Fristad, Shaver, & Holderle, 2002). Within clinical samples, the rates of depression in children range from 13–15%. Children are at increased risk if there is depression in a parent or other family history. While some attribute the rise in anxiety and depression to lower social connectedness and more environmental threats, the origin may also be genetic or idiopathic.

Supporting depressed and anxious children in school is not always easy. After all, everyone experiences some degree of sadness and nervousness. Without the expertise of an on-site psychologist or social worker, teachers and administrators must first be aware of significant problems and then devise ways to help children cope. Criteria for identifying children who may be excessively depressed or anxious are presented in Figure 6.2.

School Stressors

School can be extremely stressful for some children. Academic demands contribute to children's anxiety. Spending up to 8 hours a day in a large group with no opportunities for privacy can feel suffocating. When class sizes are especially large and classmates regularly engage in disruptive or

Figure 6.2. Childhood Depression and Anxiety

Signs of Childhood Depression
Adapted from Berk (2005) and Copeland (2001)

- Discernable sadness
- Loss of pleasure and interest in activities
- Withdrawal from people, routines, or both
- Deterioration in school performance
- Disturbances in sleep and appetite
- Difficulty concentrating
- Low energy
- Restlessness
- Expressions of hopelessness
- Excessive neediness and clinginess
- Increased irritability
- Aggressive behavior

Signs of Anxiety in Children
Adapted from Bourne (2000)

- Shortness of breath
- Heart palpitations
- Trembling
- Muscle tension
- Sweating
- Nausea or abdominal stress
- Excessive worrying
- Restlessness
- Irritability
- Disturbed sleep
- Difficulty concentrating
- Reluctance to participate or transition in routine activities

destructive behavior, anxiety levels can rise. Activities that take place outside the structure of the classroom, such as specials, lunch, recess, and hallway passing, can be especially difficult for children who need quiet and order. While most children easily adapt to the noisy, fast-paced, and sometimes chaotic routines of the school day, teachers and administrators must recognize the impact of these potential stressors on individual children. They also need to examine their possible role in exacerbating the stress in the classroom.

Hailey is a child who requires special attention to reduce her apprehension throughout the day. It would be useful to have one adult greet Hailey every morning and ease her entry into the building and her classroom. A consistent individual demonstrating caring and support would ideally build Hailey's confidence and her ability to independently transition into school. Hailey had already removed herself from school lunch and recess by refusing to go. However, supervision of Hailey during this daily period was not sufficiently planned, resulting in uncertainty for her. A set schedule for where Hailey is to go every day would be reassuring and ultimately beneficial. The adult who spends one-on-one time with Hailey could initiate communication in a gentle and compassionate manner. Teaming her up with one child who can act as a buddy may also serve as a bridge to her peers. Distinctive experiences like these, which are sensitive to children's needs, are necessary to ensure that each child thrives in the school environment.

RACIAL ISSUES

Aaliyah is a first-grade student in a suburban elementary school. The population is fairly homogeneous, with the majority of students being White. Aaliyah, who is African American, went home upset about comments that her classmates made to her earlier that day. They said that her hair was funny and that her skin looked dirty. In response, her mother immediately went to the principal, asserting that her daughter was the victim of racism.

Children are cognizant of physical differences and often mention these disparities when engaged in conversation. It is not always easy to determine if comments such as those made to Aaliyah are benign rather than intentionally hurtful. Aaliyah's classmates, through their own observations, may be merely delineating variations in physical appearance rather than making discriminatory remarks. Developmentally, they may not be aware that their words are insulting or racist. First graders have not yet fully developed social skills such as good judgment, impulse control, the ability to reflect, and a sense of the possible consequences their words may have.

Children often lack regular exposure to culturally diverse people when growing up in suburbia. They may only interact with children who look like them, speak the same language, and come from similar economic backgrounds. Tolerating or, better yet, appreciating differences has to be taught and modeled initially at home and, later on, at school and in the broader community.

Racism is an uncomfortable topic about which people are often afraid to talk. Despite how far this society has come in the battle against racism, in many cases people who act or look different are often perceived as threatening. For example, those who speak with an accent or dress in a unique style based on religious beliefs may be teased, rejected, or even scapegoated. In mainstream culture, standards of beauty are generally defined as "White" and those who come from different cultures are often compared and measured based on that standard (Wiseman, 2002). Clearly, in the elementary school world, where children are jockeying for position in various social groups, looking different can lead to insults and ostracism. The pressure to conform and maintain a sense of belonging to the group can perpetuate acts of cruelty, even if to commit such acts requires relinquishing empathy and kindness. In a sense, the unwritten rules may require children to act in ways that are not recognizable, and actually to contradict their belief system. Group members can use words as weapons and as a means of asserting power against outsiders. While teasing and name-calling are universal pursuits of both young and old, certain insults cross the line, making the victim feel worthless and humiliated. Thompson and Grace (2001) consider name-calling the verbal equivalent of physical fighting. While preschoolers rely on comments such as "I hate you" or "You're stupid," school-agers resort to more sophisticated

verbal barbs. A child's status may rise on the basis of the quality of his or her "put-downs." The media models this style of interacting through situation comedies on television in which children "learn it is funny to be insulting" (Thompson & Grace, 2001, p. 108).

Responding to Children's Insensitivity

Regardless of whether the comments made to Aaliyah were racist or innocent, there needs to be a response. Even if the teacher witnessed the offensive remarks firsthand, she might choose to carefully observe additional interactions between the children before intervening. Of course, if Aaliyah approached the teacher for assistance, an immediate reaction would be necessary. Before automatically reprimanding the other children, the teacher would want to better understand the context of the remarks. With Aaliyah by her side, she would approach the group and question the children about what was said. Through this conversation, the teacher would be enlightened about what factors are operating:

- Were the children trying to hurt Aaliyah?
- Were they merely curious about her physical appearance?
- Is there an undercurrent of racism or intolerance in the classroom?
- Was Aaliyah being overly sensitive?

To begin to answer these questions, the teacher needs to first step back and assess the cultural climate of the classroom. Part of this investigation includes a self-study to identify one's own biases (Kolozak, 2004). Everyone has biases. Being cognizant of them will prevent their intrusion into one's practice. When teachers go through an introspective process, they can create an environment in which fairness and equity are mainstays of the curriculum. As discussed previously, the teacher might implement a social skills curriculum that proactively addresses issues of diversity and respect for others. A shared language and mutually agreed-upon rules built into the curriculum can circumvent the teasing, name-calling, and hurtful comments that are so common among students. Most important, students from diverse backgrounds should be empowered to express themselves and handle social challenges within the classroom setting. Teachers need to help children engage in a dialogue that appraises differences objectively and values uniqueness, individual beauty, and identity. Each child might be asked to draw his or her self-portrait, followed by a discussion about the physical characteristics and traits that make each child special. A role-play situation in which children practice various scenarios could help them feel more prepared to counter negative or hurtful statements. To cultivate positive feelings, the teacher might ask the students to write something that they like about each of their classmates. Aaliyah, in particular, could benefit from some strategies on how to respond individually to her classmates' questions and observations. These include walking away from unpleasant conversations or using humor to defuse negativity. Knowing when to ask for help from an adult is another important coping skill.

Valuing cultural diversity in the classroom needs to be an ongoing focus. Teachers must develop curricula that go beyond a superficial multicultural approach (Phillips, 1994). Just paying token recognition to other cultures during Black History Month, Chinese New Year, or Cinco de Mayo is nothing but a "tourist curriculum." Derman-Sparks (1989) talks about the need for an antibias curriculum that integrates diversity into the physical environment, books, materials, and learning activities.

Aaliyah's teacher might develop activities that specifically address the issues in her classroom. A sample lesson plan is presented in Figure 6.3. As demonstrated by the sample lesson, a meaningful dialogue raising awareness about racial differences can easily be initiated. Teachers do not need extensive materials or training to raise children's consciousness and increase their cultural sensitivity. Respecting diversity and acknowledging similarities is an important ingredient for building communities.

Children need to see themselves represented in literature, pictures, and discussions throughout the year. On an ongoing basis, leaders and parents from various ethnic groups might be invited to talk to children about their careers and life experiences to serve as role models for all children.

Aaliyah's mother is understandably upset for her daughter. Her concerns need to be addressed, even if it turns out that she has overreacted. The faculty needs to share their understanding of the

Figure 6.3. "Accepting the Sneetches" Lesson Plan

Goal
The goal of this lesson is to help students learn to appreciate racial differences.

Objectives
- Students will interpret the meaning of Dr. Seuss's story, "The Sneetches."
- Students will talk with one another about physical differences.
- Students will be more sensitive in their interactions.

Materials
- The book "The Sneetches and Other Stories" by Dr. Seuss (Geisel, 1961)
- Blank paper
- Crayons and markers
- Chart paper and marker

Time Frame
1 hour total—about 40 minutes for a read-aloud of the book, a discussion, and a drawing activity; students will share their drawings on the following day, which should take no longer than 20 minutes.

Procedure
1. In a whole-group setting, the teacher reads the first story in the book, "The Sneetches" (pp. 1–25).
2. Throughout the reading, the teacher checks for understanding with questions such as
   a. Why were the Star-Belly Sneetches unkind to the Plain-Belly Sneetches?
   b. How do you think the Plain-Belly Sneetches felt about being left out?
   c. Why do you think the Plain-Belly Sneetches wanted stars on their bellies?
   d. Is it better to have plain bellies or stars on your bellies?
   e. In the end, how did the Sneetches "get smart"?
3. Following the reading, the children are asked to think about and then discuss why the teacher chose this book.
4. The teacher makes certain that the children understand the moral of the story before proceeding to the next step.
5. Children are asked to independently draw a picture of a scene in the book that they find most hurtful. Students work at their desks.
6. On the following day, the teacher gathers the whole class into the meeting area. Students are asked to share their pictures, telling why someone in their scene was hurt.
7. Teacher charts students' responses, noting patterns.
8. The teacher asks the children what they learned from the book and the sharing of their drawings.

Homework
Students are assigned the task of discussing the book with their parents.

Modifications for Special Needs/Differentiated Instruction
Larger crayons are provided for children with fine-motor difficulties. Students who are able to write are encouraged to add text to their artwork.

Evaluation
Teacher will discern the effectiveness of this lesson by observing students' willingness to talk about racial differences and the quality of their subsequent interactions.

situation and at the same time clarify what is developmentally appropriate in first grade. They would communicate about what steps are being taken to build a classroom community that promotes tolerance and mutual respect. Most important, the teacher must convey that Aaliyah's emotional well-being is a priority. The faculty would pledge to be vigilant in their observations of Aaliyah and her classmates and act accordingly if there were any overt signs of racism.

GIFTED CHILDREN

James is an extremely bright fifth grader. Despite being given additional work, he often complains that he is bored. During lessons, he will either read a nonrelated book or call out answers before other students have a chance. James laughs when other children make mistakes and says, "That's so easy." He is quick to correct his teacher in front of the class and will barrage her with questions to prove her wrong. James frequently gets into struggles with peers during recess and gym class, as he always strives hard to be first and best. James's parents are informed when he is unkind to peers and disrespectful to teachers, but they attribute his difficulties to an ineffective curriculum that does not address his giftedness.

James's boredom in school is a serious issue. It is not the only reason he has social difficulties, but is nevertheless a factor. A child like James, who is hard to challenge academically, is a familiar figure in today's classroom. He completes his work at a rapid pace, always seems to know the answers, and dominates small-group and classroom discussions. James has a hard time fitting in with peers in part because he is so different from them, cognitively and behaviorally. He makes sure everyone knows how smart he is, which can present as arrogance. It is common for exceptionally bright students to feel bored and subsequently resentful that they do not get enough of their teachers' attention. Gifted children may be seen as having behav-

ior problems because they can be uncooperative and resistant to routines (Clark, 2002).

Teachers and administrators typically do not receive sufficient training in educating the gifted and talented and may not know how to address these children's special needs. A 1996 survey by the National Research Center on Gifted and Talented found professional development in gifted education to be quite limited (Westberg, Burns, Gubbins, Reis, Park, & Maxfield, 1998). The researchers indicated that school districts spend just 4% of their professional development budget on in-service related to gifted education. With increased pressure on schools for students to meet minimal levels on standardized tests, attention turns to the weaker students. Teachers take for granted that their most capable students excel without individualized attention or modifications. School can be dreadful for students who find the work too easy and are not intellectually stimulated. It is not surprising that between 15% and 40% of children identified as gifted on standardized tests are considered underachievers (Seeley, 1993). Using a broader definition of giftedness, it is estimated that up to 85% of gifted students are underachievers (Sisk, 1987; Whitemore, 1980).

When identifying gifted children, educators rely on criteria defined by researchers, theorists, and organizations. With the development of the Stanford-Binet test in 1921, giftedness corresponded with intelligence; a child with an IQ of 140 and above (or the top 2% of the population) was considered gifted (Terman, 1925). In 1972, the commissioner of education published a report to Congress (Marland, 1972), which included multiple traits to define the concept. Children who show potential or outstanding achievement in at least one of the following six categories is considered gifted: general intellectual ability, specific academic aptitude, creative or productive thinking, leadership ability, ability in visual art or the performing arts, or psychomotor ability. Renzulli (1978) distinguished giftedness as a state, rather than a permanent trait: children can be gifted in particular venues but not necessarily all the time. According to Renzulli, three characteristics must be observed for a child to be considered gifted: above-average ability, creativity, and task commitment. Like Marland's definition, Renzulli's concept is broad and identifies more children than when a single measurement of intelligence on a standardized IQ test is used. Concerned that *gifted* had become an elitist term, the U.S. Department of Education (Ross, 1993) refined its criteria to take into account children who exhibit a talent at a higher level than those of their peers. It implied that there was a continuum of talent, and therefore even more children were entitled to gifted education services. Depending on the definition, gifted and talented students constitute 10% to 25% of the population (Clark, 2002).

While individuals express their exceptionality in a variety of ways, the following characteristics are commonly seen in a child considered a gifted learner:

- Asks questions
- Is highly curious
- Is intellectually engaged
- Has original ideas
- Performs with ease
- May need less time to excel
- Responds with detail and unique perspectives
- Manipulates information
- Creates new and original products
- Is beyond her or his age peers
- Needs 1 to 2 repetitions for mastery
- Constructs abstractions
- Draws inferences
- Initiates projects
- Is an innovator
- Is insightful; makes connections with ease
- Is intense
- Shows strong feelings, opinions, perspectives
- Thrives on complexity
- Is highly self-critical (Heacox, 2002, p. 136)

Meeting the Needs of the Gifted

Educational methods for gifted and talented students run the gamut from once-a-week pull-outs to full-time tracking. Currently, many experts in the field advocate for differentiation of instruction (Benjamin, 2003; Gregory & Chapman, 2002; Heacox, 2002; Tomlinson, 1999, 2001, 2003). Differentiated instruction is an ideal strategy for classes that are heterogeneously grouped; that is, placing children of differing abilities together. Differentiation involves making modifications not only for children with learning disabilities but also for the brightest

children. Students who need challenges are given alternative assignments, not just additional work.

In order to individualize instruction, teachers preassess children before beginning any unit of study and also measure development along the way. This knowledge of students' abilities influences the content, level, and pace of the lessons. Traditionally, assessment takes place at the end of a period of learning to determine what information students have memorized or internalized; a grade is given, and the class moves on to the next topic. Ongoing assessment is not used for the purpose of grading but instead to clarify the students' needs. Assessment need not be in the form of an exam. Teachers can gauge students' progress through oral questioning and discussions, reflective writing pieces, and even homework. Some teachers use "exit cards" (Tomlinson, 1999) at the end of each class as a quick evaluation. Students are given one short problem to solve that reflects the skills or concepts covered that day.

In differentiated classrooms, educators tier their lessons and teach in small groups, at three different levels (Tomlinson, 2003). Groups are flexible so that they are not always homogeneous. Students may be grouped by interest and by learning style, randomly or intentionally balanced with individual strengths and weaknesses. Curriculum compacting (Heacox, 2002) is sometimes used in classes to allow children who have already mastered the skills and concepts in a given unit to engage in alternative work. Children who demonstrate competence in a given subject through preassessment undertake higher-level work, sometimes through guided, independent studies, and interest-based investigations. Compacting eliminates unnecessary repetition for children.

When James's struggles in school are explored, it becomes clear that he needs support in both the social and academic realms. His behavior with both peers and adults may very well stem from boredom in the classroom, but challenging work will not simply make him socially adept. James's teacher must provide him with stimulating learning experiences and at the same time direct his interactions positively. Including James's parents in this process is critical, as they can provide insight about how James feels and also support the efforts of the teacher.

There are several ways that James's teacher can challenge him and other children with above-average ability. Teaching tiered lessons in small groups would enable her to match the curriculum to different ability levels. As previously stated, it is best to also regularly group students heterogeneously to avoid tracking or labeling within the class. Teachers can modify readings, assignments, and assessment with relative ease. For example, if the class was studying the human muscular/skeletal system in science, and James was already an expert, instead of reading and answering questions on basic material, he could be given higher-level reading or assigned research comparing the muscular/skeletal systems of humans and apes. The assignment would be graded according to a rubric with which James was familiar. The rubric shown in Figure 6.4 was created for James to clarify expectations about a research report.

Assuming that math was an area of strength for James, he would be given more complex problems applying the same skills the class was learning. If

Figure 6.4. Research Report Rubric

CATEGORY	4	3	2	1
Organization	Information is organized with well-constructed paragraphs and subheadings.	Information is organized with well-constructed paragraphs.	Information is organized, but paragraphs are not well constructed.	The information appears to be disorganized.
Amount of Information	All topics are addressed and all questions answered with at least two sentences about each.	All topics are addressed and most questions answered with at least two sentences about each.	All topics are addressed, and most questions answered with one sentence about each.	One or more topics were not addressed.
Quality of Information	Information clearly relates to the main topic. It includes several supporting details and/or examples.	Information clearly relates to the main topic. It provides one to two supporting details and/or examples.	Information clearly relates to the main topic. No details and/or examples are given.	Information has little or nothing to do with the main topic.
Sources	All sources (information and graphics) are accurately documented in the desired format.	All sources (information and graphics) are accurately documented, but a few are not in the desired format.	All sources (information and graphics) are documented, but many are not in the desired format.	Some sources are not accurately documented.
Mechanics	No grammatical, spelling, or punctuation errors.	Almost no grammatical, spelling, or punctuation errors.	A few grammatical, spelling, or punctuation errors.	Many grammatical, spelling, or punctuation errors.
Notes	Notes are recorded and organized in an extremely neat and orderly fashion.	Notes are recorded legibly and are somewhat organized.	Notes are recorded.	Notes are recorded only with peer/teacher assistance and reminders.
First Draft	Detailed draft is neatly presented and includes all required information.	Draft includes all required information and is legible.	Draft includes most required information and is legible.	Draft is missing required information and is difficult to read.
Paragraph Construction	All paragraphs include introductory sentence, explanations or details, and concluding sentence.	Most paragraphs include introductory sentence, explanations or details, and concluding sentence.	Paragraphs include related information but are typically not constructed well.	Paragraphing structure is not clear and sentences are not typically related within the paragraphs.
Graphic Organizer	Graphic organizer or outline has been completed and shows clear, logical relationships between subtopics.	Graphic organizer or outline has been completed and shows some logical relationships between subtopics.	Graphic organizer or outline has been started and includes some topics and subtopics.	Graphic organizer or outline has not been attempted.

students were first learning about decimals, James could be asked to make a chart listing equivalent fractions, decimals, and percentages. Note that James is given alternative class work, rather than more material on the same level. Children who are gifted do not necessarily want to do more than the rest of the class.

Assessing James before and during units of study will direct his teacher's instructional goals. If she senses that James is fairly competent on a particular topic, she can give him the end of the unit exam ahead of time. This allows her to ascertain any relative weakness and then focus on developing that knowledge or concept. James could possible ace an exam, which would indicate that he is ready to explore a related topic or the same one in more depth.

Another means of differentiating the curriculum in James's class is through learning centers. The term *learning center* is sometimes used to describe an area within the classroom. For example, the class library may be called a reading center. Manipulatives are kept in the math center, while microscopes and magnifying glasses are found in the science center. However, learning centers are actually evolving activities related to a current theme, not just objects. Teachers create hands-on opportunities to reinforce skills, explore concepts, and apply classroom learning to real-life problems. Students work independently or in small groups. Most important, centers include tasks at different levels. These tiered assignments can be sequential, meaning students must complete Activity A before going on to Activity B. Children who are cognitively advanced, like James, might be directed to begin with Activity C. Learning-center activities are typically enjoyable and serve to motivate all the children in the class. The learning center shown in Figure 6.5, which focused on the American Revolution, was developed in James's class.

Although James's school does not have a separate gifted program, teachers and administrators can initiate lunchtime enrichment clubs. Clubs are open to all students, and because they are self-selective, they will appeal only to those students who desire additional challenge. Teachers volunteer or are paid a stipend to facilitate learning groups on topics such as Debating for Democracy, Brain Boosters (Barlow, 1997), Fun with Tangrams, Baseball Math, and Inventions and Innovations.

Figure 6.5. The American Revolution Learning Center

Colonial America

Go to *www.scholastic.com/profbooks/netexplorations/index.htm* for the following activities:

Activity A Define the words *bayonet, cavalry, duty, loyalist, militia, minutemen, parliament, patriot*

Activity B Interpret the meaning of the song "Yankee Doodle."

Activity C Choose three famous quotes from the Web site and explain why they are significant. Then write your own quote.

Important Documents

Activity A What is a treaty? What purpose do you think a treaty serves? Name four to six facts regarding the Treaty of Paris.

Activity B Bill of Rights crossword puzzle.

Activity C Rewrite an article of the U.S. Constitution in plain language

People of the Revolution

Activity A When was Paul Revere's ride? What was the purpose of his ride? Which towns did he pass through? How did Revere's ride end?

Activity B Choose three of the following women and describe their role in the American Revolution: Deborah Samson, Margaret Corbin, Molly Hays McCauley, Anne Bailey, Nancy Morgan Hart.

Activity C Describe the leadership qualities of George Washington. How did his prior work prepare him for the presidency? How would you compare his leadership to that of our current president?

Providing challenges that match James's capabilities is essential, but it is only part of the intervention. James also needs help in recognizing how his behavior is perceived and how it relates to his conflicts with peers. His teacher, an administrator, or psychologist could spend some time with James discussing observed interactions, his feelings, and those of his peers. These one-on-one sessions may be enough to motivate James to be more sensitive to others. It is possible that James was just looking for attention. However, it is also possible that James's troubles are more complex, and his parents' involvement would be necessary. When James's parents express their belief that he only has difficulties because he is bored, James's teacher would share her concern that this message to their son may be unintentionally fueling the problem.

James may have come to the conclusion that his boredom is justification for his behavior. Helping James to be reflective and take responsibility is a key step in improving his social interactions. The concept of emotional intelligence (Goleman, 1995) would be shared with James and his parents to help them understand the importance of getting along with others. Goleman suggests that success in life is not determined by IQ but by one's ability to work cooperatively with others.

CONCLUSION

Developmental discipline can help children improve their emotional intelligence by encouraging them to look inside themselves and ask some key questions: What is working and what is not working? What do I want? What do I have to do to get what I want? Am I happy with how I behave? What can I do differently? Being reflective is not easy for children or adults. However, it is a stepping-stone toward accountability. This is the ultimate goal: for children to see themselves in control of their own behavior. To guide them toward that goal, we recommend that teachers do the following:

- Support parents' efforts to create a conducive homework environment
- Look for the positives in all children
- Be cognizant of signs of anxiety and depression in children
- Model respect, acceptance, and appreciation of diverse cultures
- Recognize one's own biases
- Differentiate the curriculum to meet the needs of all students and all learning styles

CHAPTER 7

Commonly Used Disciplinary Practices: How Effective Are They?

Mr. Franco is teaching a math lesson to his sixth-grade class. Several students are not paying attention, are disruptive, and are in and out of their seats. Mr. Franco announces that this is the worst class he has ever had, and they will never make it to algebra. When Austin gets up to get a tissue, he taps on every one's desk as he passes by. Mr. Franco tells Austin that he is very annoying and to stop being the class clown. The other students laugh at this exchange. Mr. Franco notices a note being passed from Kayla to Danny. He grabs the note from Danny and proceeds to read it aloud.

TEACHER INTERVENTIONS

Teachers may have the best of intentions when they attempt to manage students' behavior, but their disciplinary strategies do not always work well. At times, they may "shoot from the hip" to curtail negative behavior without being cognizant of the possible ramifications. Other times, they rely on previously used methods, such as taking away recess, sending a child out of the classroom, or coercing apologies. Educators may even resort to sarcasm or humor to win students over so that the latter follow directions. We propose, however, that these commonly used strategies do not specifically address the problem and therefore do not have a lasting impact. Moreover, teachers may inadvertently hurt children with their words, tone, or actions.

Mr. Franco has a unique style of interacting with his students. He has high expectations for his students' performance and little tolerance for misbehavior. He has been known to reduce children to tears when they forget their homework or are not paying attention. He will rebuke and even embarrass them publicly. Yet many students find Mr. Franco personable and entertaining because he has a sarcastic wit that can stimulate the group process. His sense of humor can be quite sophisticated, and as sixth graders, they appreciate being treated less as children and more as adults. It is not always clear to students how far they can go with their own humor and teasing.

Students who have a particularly difficult time in Mr. Franco's class are those who struggle academically or are particularly sensitive. Being called on by any teacher can be scary. However, anticipating that Mr. Franco might make a derogatory comment is terrifying to some. For children who are impulsive and lack self-control, Mr. Franco's class is a constant struggle. A student such as Austin who may have an excess amount of energy, or purposefully calls attention to himself may have trouble adhering to Mr. Franco's standards. After all, Mr. Franco's primary focus is on math and not on teaching children to behave. When instructing students, particularly in this emotionally vulnerable age group, one needs to consider how physical growth and hormonal changes influence learning. Pubescence is a period characterized by monumental physiological and psychological changes, which create uncertainty and anxiety in the developing adolescent. Brain-based research has demonstrated differences between boys and girls in learning during the preadolescent years. Boys get bored more easily than girls and tend to act out in ways that are disruptive (Gurian & Henley, 2001). They need more physical space and must move around more to harness their impulsivity. Just trying to stay in their seat for an extended period of time is a challenge. Boys tend to be louder and more prone to attention-seeking behavior, resulting in more teacher focus. Both girls and boys experiencing cognitive and physical changes may choose different behaviors to mask the uncertainty of feelings that are out of control; children may dumb themselves down, not raise their hands, or use bravado and humor and overly dominate discussions to prove themselves. According to Gurian and Henley, during this turbulent period of development, sexual feelings and psychosocial maneuvering for position in the group are more operative than actual learning. Given the behavioral challenges that Mr. Franco has experienced in his classroom, it is extremely likely that his students may be struggling with these developmental issues. Other possible causes of misbehavior in Mr. Franco's classroom are overly complex content, inconsistent messages regarding behavioral expectations, and middle school work overload.

Humiliation

Regardless of the cause of misbehavior, humiliating students has absolutely no place in the classroom. While sharing Kayla's note with the entire class may result in fewer notes being passed around, the pain of exposure to one's peers can be tremendous, especially when children are trying so desperately to fit in. The ensuing laughter from classmates is another indicator of the tenor of this classroom: Children may be nervous that they will be picked on next, and joining the group, even in cruelty, provides some degree of safety and anonymity. Teachers sometimes employ strategies to extinguish negative behaviors, without consider-

ing the impact of these measures on the overall social environment. Assigning extra seatwork or homework, removal of a much-needed break or privilege are examples of such measures. After all, teachers need to respond immediately. However, this process should ideally include observation, reflection, and weighing the variables. Part of this procedure involves anticipating how students might respond to the discipline. Will my words and actions hurt a child or instead motivate him or her to do the right thing? Students will generally behave better and learn more successfully when they feel respected and that it is safe to make mistakes, both academically and socially. Interventions can shape behavior without shame. For example, a firm hand on Austin's shoulder to quietly guide him back to his seat or a private conference with Kayla after class might be the most effective and least punitive way of communicating the desired behavior. Providing some clear, specific guidelines of what is acceptable behavior might also be helpful here as growing youngsters test their new social skills. Acknowledging, accepting, and working developmentally with this energetic age group includes building in stretch breaks; tension-release activities both in and out of the classroom; increased small-group work; and responding with patience, consistency, and firmness.

Mr. Franco may not be even be aware of how his demeanor may be affecting his students. Yet certain students have complained to their parents about their treatment, and Mr. Franco's teaching style has been brought to the attention of the administration. However, his longevity within the school, exceptional content knowledge, and unique reputation among his colleagues has shielded Mr. Franco from professional censure.

Teacher Supervision

Formal observation of teachers by administrators, mentors, or supervisors must be a part of ongoing professional development. Whether a teacher is a novice or has years of experience, pedagogical skills and teaching style need to be reviewed, modified, and updated. This is no easy task given the extensive responsibilities and time constraints of administrators. Effective administrators prioritize supervision and recognize that providing ongoing feedback and support are essential for successful schools.

The form for Observation of Teacher's Disciplinary Practice (see Appendix G) was developed to assist administrators, supervisors, mentors, and coaches in documenting their observations of teachers in the classroom. It looks at the overall classroom social-emotional environment, teacher's tone, relationships with children, and strategies employed to modify behavior. This form may be used several times over the course of the year to measure growth and to construct goals and objectives in a personalized professional-development plan. The form can be used in conjunction with anecdotes and the Teacher's Self-Reflection Inventory (refer to Appendix D).

TIME-OUT

Andy is a high-energy 5-year-old who has trouble sitting still in his kindergarten class. Typically, he interrupts group lessons by poking classmates, calling out without raising his hand, and getting up from his seat or spot on the rug. Andy complies when his teacher asks him to sit down quietly but continues to be restless. He is frequently sent to the "time-out chair," although it seems to have no impact on his behavior.

Time-out is a practice that has been the traditional "go-to strategy" when negative behavior persists. Simply defined, it involves removing a child from a conflict situation. Children are invited back when a particular time interval has passed or the teacher believes that the child will not resume the behavior. Variations range from putting the child in a specific quiet area or "thinking chair," having the child sit on the periphery of the group, or sending him or her to a corner or hallway. Time limits also vary, with one rule of thumb being one minute per age of child. In upper elementary and middle school, the method may no longer be referred to as *time-out*, but children are nevertheless separated from their peers and activities. It is more likely that they will be spending time alone in the hallway.

Teachers use time-out for a variety of reasons: disruptive behavior, inappropriate interactions, and even calling out. For some children, one epi-sode in time-out is sufficient to extinguish the negative behavior. In most cases, however, teachers resort to the repeated use of this strategy, which can reduce its power. Also contributing to time-out's ineffectiveness is that children are left for extended periods. When unattended, children often forget why they were sent away in the first place. Boredom or the desire to seek attention may then compel children to get into additional trouble. Materials may be torn off bulletin boards or books randomly pulled from shelves for entertainment. These behaviors may then continue to disturb the ongoing group, as attention is called outside of the lesson. Time-out is also ineffective when a child feels rejected by the teacher. Teachers must be careful to observe the child's reactions to be certain that time-out is not hurtful, embarrassing, or perceived as a punishment. Gartrell (2001, 2002) asserts that time-out only serves to shame and confuse children, rather than offer problem-solving skills that will benefit them in the long run. Time-out only works when a child is removed from the lesson or activity in which he or she was disruptive. When used for unrelated causes, such as tardiness or incomplete homework, children do not make a connection between their behavior and the consequence.

Andy's behavior is not atypical for a kindergartener. For children of this age, sitting quietly over an extended period is just too much to ask. Andy is apparently an active child who is not yet developmentally ready to stay still, and circle time can be a nightmare for him. It is unclear what Andy is learning by being sent out of the circle. Putting him in the time-out chair clearly has no enduring impact on his behavior because he cannot physically do what is expected of him.

Teacher's Role

Missing from the preceding scenario is the essential component of the teacher's role. When Andy is given time-out, he is all alone. He may be thinking about his after-school soccer lesson or his new video game and not the behavior that precipitated his removal. His teacher should speak to Andy to reinforce the desired behavior. Her presence will affirm that he is not being ostracized from the group and, primarily, that he is supported and not rejected by her. By speaking with Andy, she will be available to assess if he has mastered or regained control and is ready to return to the lesson. Andy would then be welcomed back calmly and his participation within the group resumed. When there is only one teacher in the classroom, it is not always possible to accompany children to time-out and discuss why they are there. However, teachers who choose to use time-out must find a way to converse with those children to evaluate how they are coping and if they are learning. If teachers are unable to promptly speak individually with children in time-out, they can remind them that they will do so as soon as possible. Some teachers use a "buddy teacher" system whereby teachers from other classrooms are on call for one another (Yang & Charney, 2005). As needed, a neighboring teacher will lend a hand by taking an especially disruptive child into her classroom.

Strategies for Effective Time-Out

The following suggestions are aimed at improving the effectiveness of time-out interventions. Reflecting on how and when time-out is used, as well as its frequency, will increase the likelihood of its success. Teachers should consider the suggestions before implementing time-out in their classrooms.

- Clarify rules, limits, and acceptable behavior to children on an ongoing basis.
- Explain that time-out is a consequence of inappropriate behavior.
- Remind children of the rules when they misbehave or act out.
- Give 1–2 warnings (at most) that if the behavior persists, a time-out will be implemented.
- Remove children from the activity or interaction, and have them sit down for a brief period.
- Determine the length of time-out based on children's age, temperament, and reactions.
- Sit down with children to enforce the procedure.
- Do not ignore children during time-out; remind them of their misbehavior and its consequences.
- Whenever possible, keep children in the environment where the incident occurred to help them remember the event that led to time-out.

- Before time-out is over, ask children to reflect on their actions and indicate that they are ready to return to the activity.
- Suspend the use of time-out if there is no change in the child's behavior.

BULLIES AND BULLYING

Lauren is miserable in third grade because one of her classmates torments her relentlessly. Michelle makes fun of Lauren's hair, her clothes, and the way she talks. Lauren's best friend is not in her class this year, and companions from previous years are no longer friendly to her. Michelle warns the other girls to stay away from Lauren or they will catch "Lauren germs." She declares that anyone who is nice to Lauren is a nerd and is not her friend. Lauren's parents have discussed the problem with Ms. Floyd, her teacher, and with the administration. Despite being repeatedly sent to the principal's office, Michelle's hurtful behavior persists.

Teasing is common behavior in childhood and does not always have malicious intent. With some groups of friends, insults are often a typical way of addressing others as well as a means of expressing humor. These children consider name-calling, using words such as "idiot," "gay," "ugly," and "bitch," to be just fooling around. When both members of a dyad or all the members of a group are accustomed to such vernacular, potentially hurtful words can be innocuous. At times, however, the teasing goes too far or a child can be especially sensitive. In these situations, the painful feelings are generally short lived, and the friends soon resume their playful verbal discourse. Because mild forms of teasing are omnipresent in childhood culture, most children are fairly resilient (Thompson & Grace, 2001). They accept the banter as a necessary by-product of being accepted within a social network.

In some cases, children are not cognizant of the power of their words. They may come from families where saying "I hate you" or "You're stupid" is perfectly normal, and they are unaware that in other families such expressions are said to be inappropriate and are prohibited. A child who is raised without exposure to negative words and phrases may be startled when confronted by them with peers. Teasing can also be damaging when it occurs between children who are not friends or expressed in a manner that conveys mockery.

When teasing occurs on a regular basis and is directed exclusively to one child, the behavior takes on a more significant meaning and is considered bullying. Bullying is defined as physical, emotional, or verbal abuse by one or more students intended to intimidate and torment a particular child (Giannetti & Sagarese, 2001). In most situations, the victim has done nothing overt to instigate the negative attention. The child may stand out because he or she looks different or acts unlike his or her peers or is from a particular racial, ethnic, or socioeconomic minority group. Bullying is not a new problem, but it appears to be increasing, as 5 million elementary and middle school students in the United States are affected (Giannetti & Sagarese, 2001). According to the National Association of School Psychologists, one in seven schoolchildren is a bully or victim.

Bullying by girls may be even more insidious than that by boys, because unlike boys, girls tend to harass within a tight network of friends, making their damage to victims more intense and harder to identify (Simmons, 2002). Girls often use backstabbing, exclusion, rumors, name-calling, and manipulation to inflict psychological pain. "Within the hidden culture of aggression, girls fight with body language and relationships instead of fists and knives" (p. 3). Their bullying is generally more cruel and more destructive, with the after effects often felt for years.

Michelle's actions toward Lauren can be qualified as bullying because her taunts are purposeful and ongoing. Lauren's show of distress not only did not end Michelle's ridicule; it perhaps fueled it. Even "getting into trouble" did not stop Michelle. She has become a revered and powerful figure in the classroom. Ms. Floyd, who has been unable to get through to Michelle, copes with the problem largely by ignoring it, unless Lauren's outcry disrupts the class. When that occurs, Michelle is sent to the principal's office, where Mrs. Alexander talks to Michelle about her behavior. Michelle promises not to do it again and is promptly sent back to class.

The School's Response

It is obvious that the discipline imposed by the school has not effected the necessary change. Too often, educators and parents rely on a limited set of disciplinary responses regardless of the behavior or its effectiveness. Repeated use of an unsuccessful strategy is problematic not only because it does not achieve the desired outcome, but also because it sends a message that rules can be broken. Michelle realizes that she can get away with being mean to Lauren. She never really gets punished, and going to Mrs. Alexander's office is no big deal to her. In fact, going to the principal's office on a regular basis has made Michelle a bit of a celebrity. Michelle seems to have the upper hand. The other students recognize that Michelle is allowed to threaten, lie, and hurt Lauren's feelings. They simultaneously resent Michelle's influence on the class and admire her courage to be defiant. These classmates are also wary that opposing Michelle would result in their being targeted as well. Preserving the status quo, or maintaining safety in numbers becomes the coping mechanism for social survival in this classroom. As for Lauren, her teachers have failed to protect her from Michelle. It may seem to Lauren that Michelle is favored, because Lauren's calls for help are not taken seriously.

Eliminating Michelle's dominance over Lauren will take considerable effort. Intervention must concentrate on Michelle, Lauren, and the other students in the class. Why do children bully? Can the bullying be prevented? What can schools do to stop a child once it has started? In order to pinpoint the issues contributing to Michelle's behavior, one must take into account the characteristics of many bullies: innate tendency toward aggression, larger physical size, lack of ego strength, and limited ability to experience guilt (Langan, 2002; Thompson & Grace, 2001). Environmental influences are also factors: exposure to violent television, movies, and video games; direct contact with violent or abusive family members; and adults' lack of responsiveness to verbal and physical aggression. In schools where students are not held accountable for their behavior and there is an absence of a social skills curriculum, bullying is more pervasive (Langan, 2002). While the experiences mentioned above do not cause children to be bullies, they are correlating features.

Exploring Michelle's background and what led her to be malicious toward Lauren must include the input of her parents. They can inform the faculty about Michelle's prior experiences in social settings involving bullying or being bullied. In addition, Michelle's parents can share Michelle's vulnerabilities; her worries, struggles, and failures. Supporting Michelle's areas of weakness is an important step in improving her behavior. Helping Lauren requires helping Michelle as well. Seeing Michelle as a troubled child, rather than as bad or evil, will facilitate the process and is particularly important when communicating with her parents. Michelle's parents must know that her teachers care about her and are optimistic about her future. Additionally, the faculty must be careful not to convey that are blaming Michelle's parents for her difficulties. As with any delicate issue, meetings with Michelle's parents necessitate planning and sensitivity. The initial focus would be on sharing observations, setting incremental goals, and brainstorming strategies. Depending on what is discovered about Michelle, recommendations would be made for specialized attention at home, additional supervision at school, social skills training, psychotherapy, a behavior management plan with concrete rewards and consequences, or a combination of these.

Creating a safe environment for Lauren is critical. Up until now, she has not been adequately protected from Michelle or the other children in the class. Repeated episodes of bullying can leave scars, literally and figuratively. Ongoing bullying strips a child of self-esteem, confidence in authority, and commitment to school. Girls who are bullied in their teens are more likely to avoid leadership roles and competition and are at risk for becoming battered women (Simmons, 2002). Lauren must know that there are structures in place within the school environment to prevent others from hurting her. This may involve restrictions placed on Michelle and any other children involved. For example, if Michelle were behaving unkindly to Lauren in the cubby area, then Michelle would not be permitted to go there when other children were present. If the abuse took place in the bathroom, those responsible would be

escorted to the bathroom until the problem subsided. Lauren needs to hear from her teachers that she is not to blame for the trouble she is experiencing and that she is a valued presence in the classroom. She would be encouraged to express her feelings regarding the situation, which may include anger at her teachers, fear, shame, and depression. At the same time, Lauren could benefit from learning social skills that would empower her to protect herself. Role-playing possible responses to a bully can help Lauren to be more assertive. She can be taught to ignore Michelle, laugh along with her, and develop comeback lines such as "Don't you have something more intelligent to say?" or "Are you still talking? I stopped listening," or "You're just being mean and nasty, and I'm not going to let you bother me." Lauren might also be asked to sympathize with Michelle by explaining that bullies are often insecure and lonely (Langan, 2002). She should also be helped to see that the other children in the classroom do not dislike her but are probably just afraid of Michelle too. Playdates and joining a school club or sports team are other avenues for integrating Lauren back into the social community. Since Lauren's emotional well-being is a priority, consideration may need to be given to moving Lauren (or Michelle) to another class.

Bystanders and Followers

While the faculty focuses on supporting Lauren and curtailing Michelle's actions, they must simultaneously address the feelings and behaviors of the other children in the class. The school's response must be both reactive to the current situation and preventative in nature to minimize the likelihood of future occurrences. Everyone in the entire classroom has been affected by Michelle's powerful role, either directly or indirectly. Classmates see Michelle in charge and the adults unwilling or unable to stop her. Peer pressure is an imposing force (Harris, 1998), and even more so when accompanied by manipulation and intimidation. Eliminating Michelle's access to Lauren is the first step in reestablishing authority and instilling a sense of order and security within the classroom. Once students understand that mistreatment of classmates is not tolerated, they can be taught to stand up to bullies and others who attempt to exert negative influence on them. In the context of small-group discussions conducted by the teacher, administrator, or mental health professional, students learn that bullies are only effective when there is an audience of followers and bystanders who do not help the victim. Without this audience, bullies are impotent. The following suggestions can be shared with students to help them when confronted with bullying:

1. Refuse to join in.
2. Walk away when bullies are acting up.
3. Distract the bully so he or she stops the bullying behavior.
4. Report any bullying you see.
5. Speak out.
6. Stand beside the bully's target.
7. Work with others to reduce bullying (Langan, 2002, pp. 41–43).

Role-playing various scenarios will develop students' communications skills and heighten their empathy and sensitivity toward others. It may also unveil a plethora of feelings that have been bottled up by the students, including frustration, helplessness, and guilt. Validating students' experiences will promote their willingness to discuss future interpersonal conflicts.

Teachers and administrators should carefully observe their students, especially in undersupervised locations such as the bathroom, cubbies, closets, playgrounds, and stairwells. Any reported incidences of bullying must be promptly addressed. An Assessment of Bullying in the Classroom/School inventory (see Appendix H) can assist educators in evaluating the prevalence of bullying in their settings. It helps the observer recall bullying behaviors and the frequency of such occurrences.

Many schools implement formal antibullying programs to provide their teachers with a concrete means of addressing this multifaceted problem. The Bully Prevention Program was selected by the Center for the Study of Prevention of Violence at the University of Colorado (cited in Giannetti & Sagarese, 2001) and considered to be highly effective. The program includes anonymous student questionnaires, teacher observations, class discussions of bullying and empathy, and school conference days to integrate strategies and development skills. Another example is the Bullyproofing Your School curriculum (Short-Camilli, 1994), which emphasizes a three-tiered platform: (1) We will not bully other students, (2) we will help others who are being bullied by speaking out and by getting adult help; and (3) we will use extra effort to include all students in activities at our school. The program involves student instruction, staff training, victim support, intervention with bullies, and working with parents. Peace Builders (peacebuilders.com) is a community-based violence prevention program that teaches basic rules: praise others, avoid put-downs, seek out wise people as advisors and friends, notice when others have been hurt, and right wrongs (Thompson & Grace, 2001). Teachers who work in schools that have used Peace Builders for 2 years note a significant improvement in students' social competence and more positive behavior patterns. Regardless of whether schools and districts develop their own antibullying curricula and policies or adopt an existing program, educators must be proactive when managing bullying.

CLASS DISRUPTIONS

Winter vacation is soon approaching, and 10-year-old Miguel is having an increasingly difficult time concentrating in school. He is more talkative and active than usual, especially when he is expected to sit still. During Ms. Ryan's geography lesson, Miguel is cracking jokes and making funny faces, causing his classmates to laugh out loud. Ms. Ryan has warned Miguel several times to be quiet and pay attention, but his attentiveness is short-lived. After Miguel's poking Marti, tickling Max, and taking Sam's pencil, Ms. Ryan announces that the class will lose recess because of Miguel's disruptions. Several students complain that they weren't doing anything wrong and that it's not fair for everyone to be punished. Ms. Ryan suggests that the class discuss it with Miguel. They proceed to yell at Miguel.

Teachers often find themselves competing for students' attention. Impending school breaks, first snowfalls, and Halloween parties, for example, can make schoolwork more arduous. For some children, trouble focusing occurs regularly—every Friday afternoon, immediately following lunch, or at the end of the school day. When special events are anticipated, talking with friends and joking around during lessons and work periods are not necessarily acts of defiance but rather restlessness and impatience. Teachers who try to conduct business as usual during these times may find their efforts to contain children's exhilaration to be futile. Ms. Ryan is having such an experience in her classroom. Despite her repeated warnings that Miguel behave appropriately, he remains disinterested and distracted.

Teachers must make a decision when they realize that they are losing or have lost students' attention. They can forge ahead, reaching some of but not all the children. Time constraints and the demands of a mandated curriculum pressure teachers to move forward regardless of the effectiveness of their instruction. When teachers opt to continue an unproductive lesson, they can either ignore inattentiveness and disruptions or invest effort and time in disciplining children. Ms. Ryan chose to correct Miguel's behavior and eventually impose a consequence on the entire class. Her actions did not facilitate her instructional goals but rather created more disorder in the classroom. If instruction is not going well, either because of behavior problems or a lack of understanding on the students' part, shifting gears is an essential strategy. Lessons can be altered, in style, presentation, or content. Teachers may need to tap dance if necessary to keep students on task. Often a brief stretch or a change in seating (e.g., moving from desks to the floor) is sufficient to reengage students. Bargaining can also work. A teacher can suggest, "Give me 5 more minutes and then we'll take a fruit break." Rather than disregarding the circumstances that distract children, a teacher's addressing them directly can lead to creative compromises. Knowing that Miguel is only thinking about vacation, Ms. Ryan could say, "Miguel, I know you're excited about winter vacation, and you're having trouble following what we are doing. Let's take the next 15 minutes to discuss our plans for the break. Then, I'll expect you to work your hardest to stay focused." Ms. Ryan could also ask the class to write a poem about how they are feeling or a play about an upcoming special activity. Students who will be traveling could calculate the distance from home to

their destination, creating an alternative geography lesson. These somewhat nontraditional approaches to misbehavior in class avoid conflict, turn negative interactions into teachable moments, and validate children's experiences. When students believe that their teachers care about what they care about, behavior is dramatically improved and learning is more successful.

No Recess

Ms. Ryan should reconsider whether taking away recess from a child who is having trouble sitting still is a logical response. Teachers regularly threaten and then remove recess from children for disruptive behavior, talking back, and not completing assignments or homework. They may assume that recess matters the most to children and therefore helps to deter them from misbehaving. That may be true, temporarily. However, children only internalize rules and develop self-control when they have experienced consequences that are directly related to their previous actions. They will do the right thing to not lose a prized privilege, but they will not do so independently of that anticipated "punishment." Recess should only be shortened if a child broke the rules during recess. Sitting out for a period of time, possibly watching the other children enjoy themselves, will help a child understand the necessity of behaving as expected. Eliminating an entire recess should be reserved for extreme circumstances when a child is physically or verbally hurtful to others. For Miguel, not being allowed to go to the playground and run around will not improve his ability to sit quietly and pay attention in class but rather increase his need to be active.

Group Punishments

Another question for Ms. Ryan to ponder is whether the entire class should be penalized for Miguel's misbehavior. The issue of fairness is profound for children, and adults have a responsibility to model and implement justice whenever possible. Teachers often think of their class as a whole and not as individual students, with the majority doing what is asked of them. It is disconcerting for a child who is well behaved to be reprimanded when he or she has done nothing wrong. Likewise, when teachers offer rewards to groups who are following directions, individual children can suffer. It is routine practice to praise or first call on the cluster of students who are cleaned up and sitting quietly. Children who are unfortunate enough to be seated in a cohort with a noisy or slow child never get the opportunity to line up first or hand out the papers. Ms. Ryan is hoping that peer pressure will persuade Miguel to calm down. In essence, she is asking the children to do what she is unable to accomplish herself. While classmates can and do influence one another's actions, it seems that in this case, the group punishment will inevitably undermine Miguel's relationships with his peers. Ms. Ryan might instead tap into the power of group dynamics in the context of a class meeting by asking students to share their feelings regarding disruptive classmates (no names, please).

COERCED APOLOGIES

Mrs. Carter is escorting her third-grade class to the school library. As they walk down the hallway, Thomas and Joe are elbowing each other. Mrs. Carter turns around and sees Joe poking Thomas and says, "Joe, you're holding up the whole class. Say you're sorry to Thomas." Joe looks toward the floor and says nothing. Mrs. Carter repeats, "Say you're sorry." There is a long pause and then Joe softly states, "I'm sorry." Exasperated, Mrs. Carter exclaims loudly, "Now say it like you mean it!" Reluctantly, Joe does as he is told, and the class proceeds to the library.

Apologies are generally viewed as necessary endings to conflicts and misbehavior. Saying "I'm sorry" is a way to express regret and subsequently receive forgiveness. Children as young as 18–24 months are taught to say "I'm sorry" when they have broken the rules. Educators ask or insist that children apologize for a variety of infractions such as talking back, being physically aggressive, or hurting someone's feelings. It is believed that if children are remorseful, they will not repeat their negative actions. Verbal or written apologies are thought to ensure that children are remorseful.

Although some discipline books espouse the importance of having children apologize (Charney, 2002; Frankel, 1996), adult-imposed apologies do little to deter future occurrences of undesirable behavior. In fact, requiring children to apologize may, ironically, have the opposite effect. Children learn early on that once they apologize, the reprimands are over. All they have to do is say the expected words, and they can resume their activities. There are no consequences. Some children become "reflex apologizers." They automatically say that they are sorry as soon as it is obvious that they are in trouble. Children may apologize even before they realize what they did wrong. While closure is desirable for both children and adults, without an understanding of the ramifications of the mistake, nothing has been learned. To the victim of mistreatment, a forced apology means that the other child got away with it.

What adults fail to recognize is that in most cases, children are not sorry for their actions. They did what they did for a reason, whether to get a desired object or to purposefully hurt another. Children may be upset that they were caught, but they are not necessarily repentant. Demanding that children say words that do not reflect how they actually feel stifles genuine communication. Teachers want to encourage children's expression and validate their feelings. They say, "It's OK to feel angry, but you may not hurt your friends," or "I understand that you are disappointed that you can't be first on line, but today is not your turn." However, when teachers tell children how they are supposed to feel (i.e., sorrow, regret), then children's authentic voices are silenced. This ultimately dissuades children from sharing their emotions. Some teachers note that they do not insist upon apologies, but instead suggest, "Don't you think you should apologize?" Asking, rather than demanding, is really no different and has the same outcome because children know exactly what is expected of them.

In the vignette given above, Joe did not "say it like he meant it" because he did not mean it. He and Thomas were just fooling around; Joe was not trying to hurt Thomas. Mrs. Carter's goal was to get her class to their special on time and did not take Joe's perspective into consideration. Her strategy was ineffective not only because Joe and Thomas were free to resume their disruptive behavior but also because Joe was pressured to lie.

Had Mrs. Carter observed more carefully and investigated the situation, she might have employed a different approach, perhaps having Joe and Thomas walk in front of her. Additional supervision was the consequence for breaking hallway rules. If the boys' behavior were an ongoing problem, they would have been in Mrs. Carter's view from the start. This simple strategy would prevent a reoccurrence of the behavior. Coerced apologies just create an illusion that the problem is resolved and does not discourage children from repeating their actions.

With young children, the words *apologize* and *I'm sorry* have little meaning. These are concepts that develop gradually over several years. Through maturation and social experiences, children acquire an ability to consider other perspectives and see the impact that their behavior has on people and situations. Freud (1966) suggests that children do not begin to experience guilt until they have completed the Oedipus stage and developed a superego, sometime after 6 years of age. Guilt and an ability to imagine other's feelings are necessary if one is to have genuine remorse. Apologies are inappropriate unless they are authentic, based on self-reflection, and an acknowledgment of personal wrongdoing.

The Value of Genuine Apologies

Although coerced apologies should be avoided, teachers are encouraged to help children reflect on and recognize their mistakes. Pointing out the harm (or potential harm) they have caused, children begin to recognize the impact of their behavior. Children should be told directly that they have hurt someone and how the other person probably feels. Whenever possible, children should be given an opportunity to make amends, not in words but in actions. An "apology of action" is an extension of a verbal apology in which children are urged to take responsibility for the harm they caused (Fillion, Garsh, Poliner, Shilalie, & Vincent, 2005). Students demonstrate their remorse by trying to rebuild the trust they have destroyed. They can be asked, "What do you think you can do to make your friend feel better?" or "How can you fix what you have done?" With guidance, children come to see that they have a responsibility to try to repair what they

have hurt or destroyed. Through experience, however, children come to see that some mistakes cannot be easily remedied. For example, gossiping and lying can permanently tarnish another person's reputation. When a child causes irreparable damage, a community service project can help give back to others in the classroom or school.

Educators can and should encourage children to acknowledge their faults. This is accomplished not by having children say the specified words, but through modeling. When children observe teachers and parents over time making mistakes and naturally apologizing for them, they come to understand the purpose of those words. Opportunities for modeling apologies happen daily: when a teacher erroneously accuses a student of not turning in homework, or blames the wrong child for misbehavior. Setting an example is a powerful mechanism that can teach children the importance of genuine apologies with little effort. Although some educators are reluctant to apologize to children for fear that it suggests weakness, it demonstrates that it is fine to err as long as one learns from the experience (Bluestein, 2001; Fields & Boesser, 2002; Mackenzie, 2003).

CONCLUSION

Regardless of the particular disciplinary strategy employed, once it has been repeated more than twice for a child, it is probably ineffective. Responding in the same way sends a message that the child can get away with the misbehavior. Teachers must also switch strategies if it hurts the child in any way. Modifying children's behavior requires continual monitoring of the intervention and a willingness to be flexible and creative. Specifically, on the basis of this chapter, we recommend that teachers do the following:

- Be cognizant of your teaching style and interactions with children
- Use time-out judiciously
- Avoid taking away children's free play or recess
- Take bullying and excessive teasing seriously
- Refrain from forcing children to apologize

CHAPTER 8

Pulling It All Together

Every educational institution has its own set of rules and standards for behavior; these reflect its underlying value system. These principles can be seen in the way children and faculty interact, resolve conflicts, and even choose to dress. Upon entering a school, one has an immediate sense about its environment, whether it is welcoming or cold, structured or chaotic, calm or tense. For a perceptive individual, a first impression can be indicative of the overall social, emotional, and educational climate of the school.

What characterizes a school that embraces developmental discipline? There are a number of qualities that distinguish developmental discipline schools. Most important, children and adults all treat one another with respect. All staff members, including custodians, aides, teachers, and administrators, speak to one another and to children and their families with kindness and sensitivity. This sets the tone for how children are expected to engage with peers and adults. Modeling is the key to creating a community of caring. What may seem so natural is in reality quite challenging. Educators are competing with the onslaught of negative messages in the media, in neighborhoods, and sometimes in families. Children are inundated with images of aggression, sexuality, profanity, and maliciousness. To safeguard schools from these influences, teachers, administrators, and parents must build an alliance. A unified commitment with high expectations and related consequences for misbehavior nurtures children as they grow.

While children in developmental discipline schools understand that they are to communicate in a positive manner, conflicts are bound to happen. Anytime people share a living space, differences in perspectives (opinions, views, values) can lead to discord. The way that individuals cope with and resolve their disagreements differentiates the developmental discipline model. Skilled observations by the faculty enable them to respond to incidents in a timely and consistent manner. Paying careful attention to the nuances of children's interactions help teachers to be proactive. Knowing that an altercation is likely to occur between certain children, a thoughtful teacher restructures the group composition, the activity, or the environment.

Because the expression of feelings and beliefs is supported, students are more apt to speak out against injustice when someone has been treated badly. They are sensitive to wrongdoing and feel empowered to affect change. Moreover, children feel that they must stand up and be heard. In developmental discipline schools, students do not tolerate bullying, hurtful teasing, or physical aggression. It takes a great deal of ego strength, courage, and support for children to resist negative peer pressure and to listen to their own inner conscience. Classroom and community meetings, discussed previously, promote the learning and expression of these skills and values. Preferably, these lessons are extended and reinforced through participation in community service. Volunteerism and fund-raising activities are opportunities to demonstrate compassion and giving on a wider scale. When these are carried out in collaboration with families, schools have a larger educational impact.

TRAINING FACULTY

Training is central to successful implementation of developmental discipline. It ensures that each staff member clearly understands the school's commitment and mission. There are ample opportunities to develop observational skills, for self-reflection, and for dialogue. Learning how to conduct productive meetings with students and facilitating role-playing are critical aspects of the training. An underlying goal of training is that educators let go of discipline practices that are either ineffective or that inadvertently contribute to the problem.

Schools will vary in their ability to dedicate time and resources to developmental discipline training. Some schools can finance the services of outside consultants, while others rely solely on administrator-led workshops and peer support. Training can take place over the summer, on faculty in-service days, during staff meetings, and at lunchtime. Ideally, the first year of implementation would consist of intense interactive learning followed by less frequent meetings in subsequent years. One variable to consider when planning is the level of experience and expertise of the faculty. It may be necessary for veteran teachers to review and update their discipline methods, while novice teachers may need to focus on the basics: teacher presence, clarification of rules, and consistent follow-through.

The suggested outline is a sequence for training faculty in the developmental discipline approach. As mentioned previously, learning must be differentiated to match the levels and needs of the participants. Therefore, educators are encouraged to modify this framework accordingly. Sessions can be repeated or extended as needed.

TRAINING SESSION 1

Goal: Whole-group introduction to developmental discipline
Topics:

- A comprehensive approach to shaping children's behavior and attitudes
- Teachers' observations of children in planning interventions
- Integrating teacher's prior knowledge of child development and professional experiences
- Taking individual children's temperament, feelings, and developmental level into account when setting expectations
- Recognizing the need for a range of discipline strategies to match the particular child and situation
- Establishing rules and consequences

TRAINING SESSION 2

Goal: Building observational skills
Topics:

- Review of various observational techniques: narrative, anecdote, checklist, rating scale, and so on
- The observational process: planning, observation, documentation, interpretation, assessment, recommendation, follow-through
- Observational methods—a practicum
- Teacher self-reflection
- Helping students examine their own behavior

TRAINING SESSION 3

Goal: How curriculum influences behavior
Topics:

- The physical environment
- Children's movement and activity
- The social-emotional environment
- The delivery of instruction
- Transitions

TRAINING SESSION 4

Goal: Creating community
Topics:

- The concept of class and community meetings
- Positive communication
- The value of role-playing
- Use of contracts
- Links to the larger community
- Facilitating group meetings—a practicum

TRAINING SESSION 5

Goal: Brainstorming and developing strategies
Topics:

- Consideration of ineffective or short-lived disciplinary strategies

- Activities/times that are most likely to trigger conflicts: transitions, recess, lunchtime, hallways, and so on
- Review and application of developmental discipline strategies (see Appendix I)

TRAINING SESSION 6

Goal: Building an alliance with families
Topics:

- The value of partnering with families
- Encouraging ongoing parent involvement in the classroom and schoolwide activities
- Sharing developmental discipline strategies to foster continuity between home and school
- Communicating observations from home and school

TRAINING SESSION 7

Goal: Integrating developmental discipline into teachers' practice (Faculty is divided into small groups based on grade, subject taught, experience level, or interest)
Topics:

- Analyzing and brainstorming solutions to behavior problems (vignettes from book or teachers' own experiences)
- Critical review of excerpts from this book and discussion
- Practicing and evaluating strategies: role-play

TEACHER CHARACTERISTICS

An overall objective of faculty training is to create consistency in practice and in attitude. While heterogeneity is an asset because individuals contribute diverse strengths, values, and perspectives, teachers and administrators should have a similar approach. The ideal teacher will use observation and reflection in order to understand each child's developmental level and needs. Maintaining sensitivity, respect, and appreciation of differences in children is an important attribute. Being attuned to oneself and the student guides teachers to the best response. Interventions can be unique and creative. Humor also helps teachers by keeping conflicts and problems in perspective. Teachers can remain true to themselves while facilitating a positive learning and social environment. Perhaps the most important characteristic of teachers who are effective in their discipline methods is an openness to learning and change. No matter how many years of professional experience, it is necessary to fine-tune one's skills and switch gears when a strategy is not working. Collaboration between faculty provides opportunities to share and brainstorm solutions. Good collegial relationships enable teachers to vent, support one another, and even make suggestions. A willingness to hear and consider constructive feedback from peers and supervisors contributes to professional success.

REACHING OUT TO FAMILIES

One of developmental discipline's primary goals is engaging parents in the process. Their input is invaluable. Consistency between home and school is as important as within the school. However, uniformity is not realistic. What is possible is sharing a commitment to the child's best interests. Without a doubt, building an alliance with some families can present a challenge. When confronted with families who disagree, are combative, or are negligent, teachers must continually focus on how best to help the child. Blaming the parents serves no purpose. Teachers need to look beyond the parents' affect and behavior to recognize their genuine love of their child. It starts with listening to family members' hopes, dreams, and expectations. When the faculty respects parents' points of view, parents are more likely to be active participants and ask for help. The door is then open for offering suggestions that will improve the child's behavior.

Educating parents about effective discipline strategies can take many forms. Parents often request workshops around issues such as helping with homework, enforcing bedtimes, and setting limits about the use of computers and television. When schools make workshops accessible to families by providing food, child care, and both day and evening meeting times, attendance is greatly increased. Tailoring workshop topics to the particular interests of the population sends a message that parents' opinions matter.

Including parents begins before the first day of school. Welcoming letters and school handbooks, which provide details about procedures, schedules, contact numbers, and curriculum, set the tone for future communication. Back-to-school night is both informative and interactive. Questions and concerns are addressed, and teachers make a pledge to be available. Phone calls, e-mails, and notes are responded to in a timely manner. Parents are encouraged to volunteer in a variety of ways: field trips, reading to the children, lunchtime supervision, and sharing of special talents and occupations. Some schools have a family lounge, which can be as simple as a room with a few chairs, a table with a pot of coffee, and access to child-rearing and educational materials.

CONCLUSION

Schools may adopt developmental discipline differently. However it is applied, what is necessary is a shared vision. Unless a school implements developmental discipline from its inception, changing philosophy and practice is an arduous process. It takes time, patience, and commitment. A willingness to self-reflect and revise attitudes and expectations goes a long way. There will be frustrations, disappointments, and inevitably successes. Small incremental steps lead to profound transformations within the school community. This journey begins and ends with observation.

Observation Training Form

Observer_____   Date_____

Directions

- Record child's name and age.
- Record observer's name and date.
- Describe the context:
  - a) physical setting
  - b) situation
- Note the time at regular intervals (include beginning and ending time).
- Record exactly what the child does in the behavioral descriptions column.
- Record your interpretations/inferences.

Child's Name_____   **Child's Age**_____

Context:

Physical Setting

Situation

Time	Behavioral Descriptions (objective)	Interpretations/Inferences (subjective)

Guidelines for Narrative Observation

Context Description
- Where does the observation take place?
- What is the physical environment like?
- Who is present during the observation? (e.g., the teacher, number of students, learning specialist, aide, visitor, administrator)
- Did anything unusual happen prior to the observation?

The Child Within the Space
- What are the expectations for the child within the physical space?
- Does the child keep his or her work area (i.e., table or desk) neat and organized?
- Does the child use communal areas (e.g., learning centers, computers, library) appropriately?

Child's Interactions with Peers
- How does the child interact with peers?
- How does the child handle conflicts?
- Does the child communicate clearly and appropriately to peers?
- How does the child respond to inappropriate behavior by others?

Child's Interactions with Adults
- Does the child communicate clearly and appropriately with teachers and other adults in the school?
- How does the child respond to the teacher's directions?
- How does the child respond to the teacher's corrections?
- Does the child have appropriate boundaries with adults?

The Learning Process
- Is the child on task?
- Does the child actively participate in the lesson?
- Does the child complete tasks within the required time?
- Does the child answer questions requiring memory and facts?
- Does the child answer questions involving critical thinking and problem solving?

Transitions
- Does the child follow directions in regards to preparing for the next activity/lesson?
- Is the child quiet and cooperative in between activities/lessons?
- How does the child behave when standing on line?
- How does the child behave in the hallways?

Narrative Observation Report

Name of Child: _____ Grade: _____ Age: _____

Date of Observation: _____ Time: _____

Observer: _____

Context Description

The Child Within the Space

Child's Interactions with Peers

Child's Interactions with Adults

The Learning Process

Transitions

Inferences

Recommendations

Peer Interaction Checklist

Name of Student _____ Grade/Class _____

Date of Observation _____ Observer _____

Setting

Overall Behavior	Observed	Not Observed	N/A
Child typically engages in positive interactions with peers.			
Child has developed appropriate and meaningful relationships with peers.			
Child demonstrates tolerance when mildly provoked.			

Comments

Small Groups Within Classroom	Observed	Not Observed	N/A
Child expresses ideas clearly to peers.			
Child demonstrates ability to listen to peers.			
Child compromises as needed for the group process.			

Comments

Unstructured Periods (Lunch, Recess, Snack Time, Transitions)	Observed	Not Observed	N/A
Child finds a place within a group.			
Child refrains from following those who are misbehaving.			
Child possesses ability to resolve conflicts peacefully.			

Comments

Teacher Self-Reflection Inventory

Name _____   Date of Observation _____

Directions: Rate each item. Think about one or two examples to support each answer.

1 = never 2 = rarely 3 = sometimes 4 = often 5 = always

Tone

My tone is positive and nonthreatening.
    1   2   3   4   5

I modulate my voice as a teaching tool.
    1   2   3   4   5

My students understand my humor.
    1   2   3   4   5

Comments

Relationships with Children

I establish relationships with the children in my class.
    1   2   3   4   5

I look at children's faces and body language to gauge their reactions.
    1   2   3   4   5

I use active listening skills with the children.
    1   2   3   4   5

Comments

Language

My students understand my vocabulary and the way I use language.
    1   2   3   4   5

I state my expectations clearly.
    1   2   3   4   5

I individualize my responses to each child.
    1   2   3   4   5

Comments

Classroom-Management Skills

I clarify classroom rules and expectations on a regular basis.
    1   2   3   4   5

I respond consistently with logical consequences.
    1   2   3   4   5

I encourage the children to communicate and problem solve.
    1   2   3   4   5

Comments

Reflections and Goals

Student Self-Reflection Inventory

Name _____ Date _____

Directions: Rate each item as 1, 2, or 3. Think about one or two examples to support each answer.

1 = rarely   2 = sometimes   3 = usually

I am good at following rules in

Class
1   2   3

Specials
1   2   3

Hallways
1   2   3

Lunch and recess
1   2   3

I am a good listener

In small-group work
1   2   3

When my teacher is teaching
1   2   3

With my friends
1   2   3

I am respectful to my

Teachers
1   2   3

Classmates
1   2   3

Other adults in school
1   2   3

Complete the following

I get in trouble because

I could do a better job in school by

My friends like me because

Something important to know about me is

Parent Observation Form

Date _____

Child's Name _____

Parent's Name _____

Choose from the following situations that are problematic for your child.
Complete one Parent Observation Form for each situation.

- Coming home from school
- Homework
- After-school activities
- Mealtime/food
- Playdates/peer interactions
- Waking up/Getting ready for school
- Travelling in the car

- Chores
- Following rules and routines
- Bedtime
- Grooming (baths, brushing teeth, toileting, dressing, etc.)
- Separations
- Sibling interactions
- Other

Problematic Situation

When It Occurs

Frequency/Duration

Observation

Your response

What do you think is really going on?

Appendix G

Observation of
Teacher's Disciplinary Practice

Teacher _____ Class _____

Observer _____ Date _____

Directions

Consider the following behaviors demonstrated by teachers, and put a check in a column for observed consistently, observed on occasion, or not observed. For each behavior not observed, support your statement with examples in the comments sections.

Social-Emotional Environment	Observed Consistently	Observed on Occasion	Not Observed
Treats children with respect.			
Takes into account children's developmental needs.			
Listens and actively encourages listening.			
Facilitates dialogue.			

Comments

Teacher Tone and Language	Observed Consistently	Observed on Occasion	Not Observed
Moderates voice according to situation.			
Looks at children when speaking to them.			
Speaks to children sensitively and at their level.			
Responds to misbehavior discretely without embarrassment.			

Comments

Relationships with Children	Observed Consistently	Observed on Occasion	Not Observed
Supports students academically.			
Is available to talk to students after class.			
Students seek out teacher for counsel.			
Is flexible in dealings with children.			

Comments

Strategies	Observed Consistently	Observed on Occasion	Not Observed
Corrects behavior consistently.			
Administers consequences that are related to the misbehavior.			
Follows through on warnings and consequences.			
Uses a variety of strategies to address children's behavior.			

Comments

Appendix H
Assessment of Bullying in the School Classroom

Date _____   **Location of Assessment** _____

Observer _____   (e.g., classroom, lunchroom, playground, hallway, bathroom, etc.)

Directions

Complete this assessment to identify incidences of bullying in your classroom and school. Teachers, specialists, administrators, aides, and parent volunteers can use this form. Fill out the form initially to determine if there is a problem and then as a follow-up every few weeks as indicated.

 Circle any of the following behaviors that you have observed directly or that have been reported to you. For every item highlighted, note the frequency of the behavior according the scale below:

√ = observed once   √√= observed more than once   √√√ = observed regularly

Teasing_____	Name-calling_____	Humiliation_____
Belittling_____	Malicious whispering_____	Spreading rumors/lies_____
Hurtful notes_____	Dirty looks_____	Manipulation_____
Scapegoating_____	Backstabbing_____	Intimidation_____
Ignoring_____	Exclusion_____	Cliques_____
Ganging up_____	Threats_____	Intentional tripping_____
Physical aggression_____	Using objects as weapons_____	Inciting others to be mean_____

Comments: (Identify all bullies and victims and describe the context of their behavior.)

Developmental Discipline Strategies

Educators are encouraged to refer to the following menu of strategies, which have been culled from the text. Selecting strategies that match one's particular style can help build a reservoir of techniques that can be adapted to various situations.

Proactive Strategies

- Observe ⟶ interpret ⟶ reflect ⟶ intervene
- Consider the child's developmental level and temperament
- Be familiar with typical and atypical developmental norms
- Recognize signs of anxiety and depression in children
- Understand the relationship between physical ailments and psychological struggles
- Create an emotionally safe environment for children
- Discourage teasing and hurtful humor among children
- Encourage listening rather than interrupting: hands down when children or teacher are speaking
- Avoid putting children in situations that might elicit undesirable behavior
- Allow children ample time to be mobile
- Anticipate aggressive behavior so it can be avoided; carefully consider group composition, seating, and line arrangements
- Monitor children's peer relationships
- Praise children for exhibiting positive behavior
- Examine your tone and length of verbalizations
- Use role-play with students to explore and express feelings and teach coping and problem solving
- Share books that help children understand and work through sensitive issues
- Encourage children to articulate their feelings
- Be cognizant of nonverbal communication
- Individualize schedules for young children
- Offer alternatives to unstructured lunchtime and recess time
- Provide individual and small-group time for children when necessary
- Adopt an antibullying/social skills curriculum

- Integrate a multicultural curriculum year-round
- Prioritize the needs of gifted children
- Have clear aisles for easy classroom movement
- Avoid shelf clutter
- Rotate materials regularly
- Create rules for the use of the environment and its materials
- Rearrange the room to suit the particular lesson
- Use voice code to monitor the noise level in the room
- Give children an activity during transition time (e.g., game or song)
- Provide children with a menu of tasks when they are finished with their work (e.g., silent reading, a problem-solving task, or completion of an unfinished assignment)
- Give ample warning prior to transitions
- Get children's attention by flicking the lights on and off, lowering your voice, or using a clapping pattern
- Conduct weekly classroom meetings
- Conduct community meetings to establish goals for the larger group
- Assign homework that is meaningful and developmentally appropriate in terms of content and length
- Individualize homework as needed
- Provide children with organizational support and study skills
- Clearly convey expectations
- Be consistent about the rules with all children
- Use external rewards, such as sticker charts, sparingly
- Model apologies when relevant
- Employ the services of consultants: psychologists, social workers, occupational therapists, physical therapists, and speech pathologists

Reactive Strategies

- Encourage children to reflect on their actions
- Change strategies that are not working
- Consequences must be individualized and relate to the infraction
- Use time-out sparingly and only if effective
- Redirect children to appropriate activities
- Teach children to use negotiation to resolve conflicts
- Empower kids to stand up to wrongdoing
- Use contracts with individuals and the whole class
- Use external reinforcement cautiously
- Separate children when negative exchanges persist
- Have children take turns with toys rather than force them to share
- Remove toys and materials when all else fails
- Provide a shadow to a child who is having trouble controlling impulses
- Ignore tantrums and whining, to extinguish the behavior
- Collaborate with colleagues and consultants to get a comprehensive perspective

Observational Techniques

- Document observations (narrative, anecdotes, frequency counts, checklists, rating scales, or a combination of these); include time, date, and context
- Observe at various times of the day and in different contexts
- Minimize bias through reflecting on understanding culture and collaboration with others
- Use videotapes to distinguish observational data from subjective interpretation
- Use clipboards, index cards, or an audio recorder to facilitate the observational process
- Share observations with colleagues

Family Outreach

- Maintain ongoing communication with families through journals, e-mails, and phone calls
- Be accessible to families; provide flexibility in scheduling meetings
- Include families in classroom activities
- Have parents conduct formal observations of their child
- Share observations with parents
- Communicate homework expectations to parents
- Maintain firm boundaries with parents
- Have a list of local referral sources

References

American Psychiatric Association. (1994). *Diagnostic and Statistical Manual of Mental Disorders* (4th ed.). Washington, DC: Author.

Anxiety Disorders Association of America. (2003). *Anxiety disorders in children and adolescents*. Philadelphia, PA: Taylor Francis.

Balaban, N. (1991). Mainstreamed, mixed-age groups of infants and toddlers at the Bank Street Family Center. *Zero to Three, 11*(3), 13–16.

Balter, L. (1985). *Dr. Balter's child sense*. New York: Pocket Books.

Bandura, A. (1963). Imitation of film-mediated aggressive models. *Journal of Abnormal and Social Psychology, 66*, 3–11.

Barlow, B. (1997). *Bob Barlow's book of brain boosters*. New York: Scholastic.

Baumrind, D. (1967). Child care practices anteceding three patterns of preschool behavior. *Genetic Psychology Monographs, 75*, 43–88.

Baumrind, D. (1991). Parenting styles and adolescent development. In J. Brooks-Gunn, R. Lerner, & A. C. Petersen (Eds.), *The encyclopedia of adolescence* (pp. 746–758). New York: Garland.

Benjamin, A. (2003). *Differentiated instruction: A guide for elementary school teachers*. Larchmont, NY: Eye on Education.

Bentzen, W. R. (2001). *Seeing young children: A guide to observation and recording behavior* (4th ed.). Albany, NY: Delmar.

Berger, E. H. (2000). *Parents as partners in education*. Upper Saddle River, NJ: Prentice Hall.

Berk, L. E. (2005). *Infants, children, and adolescents* (5th ed.). Boston: Pearson.

Bluestein, J. (2001). *Creating emotionally safe schools*. Deerfield Beach, FL: Health Communications.

Bondy, E., & Ketts, S. (2001). Like being at the breakfast table: The power of classroom morning meeting. *Childhood Education, 77*(3), 144–149.

Bossard, J. H. S., & Boll, E. S. (1966). *The sociology of child development*. New York: Harper & Row.

Bourne, E. J. (2000). *The anxiety-phobia workbook* (3rd ed.). Oakland, CA: New Harbinger.

Brady, K., Forton, M. B., Porter, D., & Wood, C. (2003). *Rules in school*. Greenfield, MA: Northeast Foundation for Children.

Brazelton, T. B. (1992). *Touchpoints: The essential reference*. Reading, MA: Addison-Wesley.

Brazelton, T. B., & Greenspan, S. I. (2000). *The irreducible needs of children*. Cambridge, MA: Perseus.

Brazelton, T. B., & Sparrow, J. D. (2001). *Touchpoints 3 to 6*. Cambridge, MA: Perseus.

Bredekamp, S., & Copple, C. (Eds.). (1997). *Developmentally appropriate practice in early childhood programs*. Washington, DC: National Association for the Education of Young Children.

Brennan, M., & Noffke, S. E. (1998). Uses of data in action research. In T. R. Carson & D. J. Sumara (Eds.), *Action research as a living practice* (pp. 23–43). New York: Peter Lang.

Bronfenbrenner, U. (1979). *The ecology of the family as a context for human development: Experiments by nature and design*. Cambridge, MA: Harvard University Press.

Browne, K. W. (2000). *Beginnings & beyond* (5th ed.). Redwood City, CA: Delmar.

Campbell, S., & Smith, K. (2001). Equity observation and images of fairness in childhood. In S. Grieshaber & G. S. Cannella (Eds.), *Embracing identities in early childhood education: Diversity and possibilities* (pp. 89–102). New York: Teachers College Press.

Carr, J. F., & Harris, D. E. (2001). *Succeeding with standards: Linking curriculum, assessment, and action planning*. Alexandria, VA: Association for Supervision and Curriculum Development.

Chan, S. (2000). Families with Asian roots. In E. Lynch & M. Hanson (Eds.), *Developing cross-cultural competence* (pp. 251–347). Baltimore: Paul H. Brooks.

Charney, R. S. (2002). *Teaching children to care: Classroom management for ethical and academic growth, K–8*. Greenfield, MA: Northeast Foundation for Children.

Children's Defense Fund. (2001). *The state of America's children yearbook*. Washington, DC: Author.

Clark, B. (2002). *Growing up gifted* (6th ed.). Upper Saddle River, NJ: Merril Prentice Hall.

Clayton, M. K. (1997). Tips for transitions. *The Responsive Classroom, 9*(3), 4–5.

Collins, C. (1995, May 11). Spanking is becoming the new don't. *The New York Times*, p. C8.

Collins, C., & Frantz, D. (1993). *Teachers talking out of school*. Boston: Little, Brown.

Copeland, M. E. (2001). *The depression workbook* (2nd ed.). Oakland, CA: New Harbinger.

Cotton, K. (2000). Schoolwide and classroom discipline. Online Journal of Northwest Regional Educational Laboratory. Available at http://www.nwrel.org/scpd/sirs/5/cu9.html.

Cummings, C. (2000). *Winning strategies for classroom management*. Alexandria, VA: Association for Supervision and Curriculum Development.

Curwin, R. L., & Mendler, A. N. (1999). *Discipline with dignity*. Alexandria, VA: Association for Supervision and Curriculum Development.

Derman-Sparks, L. (1989). *Anti-bias curriculum: Tools for empowering young children*. Washington, DC: National Association for the Education of Young Children.

DeVries, R., & Van, B. (1994). *Moral classrooms, moral children: Creating a constructivist atmosphere in early education*. New York: Teachers College Press.

Dow, S. P., Sonies, B. C., Scheib, D., Moss, S. E., & Leonard, H. L. (1999). Practical guidelines for the assessment and treatment of selective mutism. In S. A. Spasaro & C. E. Schaefer (Eds.), *Refusal to speak: Treatment of selective mutism in children* (pp. 19–44). Northvale, NJ: Jason Aronson.

Dreikurs, R., & Grey, L. (1968). *A new approach to discipline: Logical consequences*. New York: Hawthorne.

Edwards, C. (2004). *Classroom discipline and management* (4th ed.). New York: John Wiley & Sons.

Ehrensaft, D. (1997). *Spoiling childhood*. New York. Guilford Press.

Elkind, D. (1988). *Miseducation*. New York: Alfred A. Knopf.

Elkind, D. (1994). *A sympathetic understanding of the child: Birth to 16* (3rd ed.). Boston: Allyn & Bacon.

Elkind, D. (2001). *The hurried child: Growing up too fast too soon* (3rd ed.). Cambridge, MA: Perseus.

Erikson, E. H. (1963). *Childhood and society*. New York: Norton.

Executive Summary of the No Child Left Behind Act of 2001. (2001). Available at: http://www.ed.gov/offices/OESE/esea/exec-summ.html

Feldman, R. S. (2002). *Understanding psychology* (6th ed.). New York: McGraw-Hill.

Ferber, R. (1986). *Solve your child's sleep problems*. New York: Simon & Schuster.

Fields, M. V., & Boesser, C. (2002). *Constructive guidance and discipline*. Upper Saddle River, NJ: Merril Prentice Hall.

Fillion, S., Garsh, L., Poliner, R., Shilalie, J., & Vincent, K. (2005). Apology of action & literacy. *Responsive Classroom, 17*(4), 6–8.

Fraiberg, S. (1959). *The magic years*. New York: Charles Scribner's Sons.

Frankel, F. (1996). *Good friends are hard to find*. Los Angeles: Perspective.

Freud, S. (1966). *Introductory lectures on psychoanalysis*. New York: Norton.

Fristad, M. A., Shaver, A. E., & Holderle, K. E. (2002). Mood disorders in childhood. In D. T. Marsch & M. A. Fristad (Eds.), *Handbook of serious emotional disturbance in children and adolescents* (pp. 228–265). New York: John Wiley & Sons.

Garbarino, J. (1995). *Raising children in a socially toxic environment*. San Francisco: Jossey-Bass.

Gartrell, D. (2001). Replacing time-out: Part 1, Using guidance to build an encouraging classroom. *Young Children, 56*(6), 8–16.

Gartrell, D. (2002). Replacing time-out: Part 2, Using guidance to build an encouraging classroom. *Young Children, 57*(2), 36–43.

Gartrell, D. (2004). *The power of guidance: Teaching social-emotional skills in early childhood classrooms*. Albany, NY: Thomson-Delmar Learning.

Geisel, T. S. (1961). *The Sneetches and other stories*. New York: Random House.

Genishi, C. (Ed.). (1992). *Ways of assessing children and curriculum*. New York: Teachers College Press.

Gestwicki, C. (2000). *Home, school, and community relations*. Albany, NY: Delmar.

Giannetti, C. C., & Sagarese, M. (2001). *Cliques: Eight steps to help your child survive the social jungle*. New York: Broadway Books.

Ginott, H. G. (1965). *Between parent and child*. New York: Macmillan.

Ginott, H. G. (1972). *Teacher and child*. New York: Macmillan.

Glickman, C. D. (2002). *Leadership for learning: How to help teachers succeed*. Alexandria, VA: Association for Supervision and Curriculum Development.

Godfrey, A. (1998). Babies, parents, and sleep. *Zero to Three, 19*(2), 3–4.

Goleman, D. (1995). *Emotional intelligence*. New York: Bantam Books.

Gordon, T. (1970). *Parent effectiveness training*. New York: Peter H. Wyden.

Gordon, T. (1976). *TET: Teacher effectiveness training*. New York: Peter H. Wyden.

Gregory, G. H., & Chapman, C. (2002). *Differentiated instructional strategies: One size doesn't fit all*. Thousand Oaks, CA: Corwin.

Greven, P. J. (1992). *Spare the child: The religious roots of punishment and the psychological impact of physical abuse*. New York: Knopf.

Griffin, A. (1994). Heart start: The emotional foundations of school readiness as challenge, lens and language for training. *Zero to Three, 15*(3), 5–10.

Gurian, M., & Henley, P. (2001). *Boys and girls learn differently*. San Francisco, CA: Jossey-Bass.

Harms, T., Clifford, R. M. S., & Cryer, D. (2005). *Early childhood environment rating scale* (Rev. ed.). New York: Teachers College Press.

Harris, J. R. (1998). *The nurture assumption*. New York: Free Press.

Heacox, D. (2002). *Differentiating instruction in the regular classroom*. Minneapolis, MN: Free Spirit.

Hinson, C. (2001). *Six steps to a trouble-free playground*. Wilmington, DE: PE.

Hobson, D. (1996). Beginning with the self: Using autobiography and journal writing in teacher research. In G. Burnaford, J. Fischer, & D. Hobson (Eds.), *Teachers doing research: Practical possibilities* (pp. 1–17). Mahwah, NJ: Lawrence Erlbaum.

Huntsinger, C. S., Huntsinger, P. R., Ching, W., & Lee, C. (2000). Understanding cultural contexts fosters sensitive caregiving of Chinese American children. *Young Children, 55*(6), 7–15.

Hyman, I. (1997). *The case against spanking*. San Francisco: Jossey-Bass.

Joe, J., & Malach, R. (2000). Families with Native American roots. In E. Lynch & M. Hanson (Eds.), *Developing cross-cultural competence* (pp. 127–164). Baltimore, MD: Paul H. Brooks.

Jones, E., & Nimmo, J. (1994). *Emergent curriculum*. Washington, DC: National Association for the Education of Young Children.

Kaiser, B., & Rasminsky, J. S. (1999). *Meeting the challenge: Effective strategies for challenging behaviours in early child environments*. Ottawa, Ontario: Canadian Child Care Federation.

Knopf, I. J. (1984). *Childhood psychopathology*. Englewood Cliffs, NJ: Prentice-Hall.

Kohn, A. (1999). *Punished by rewards*. New York: Houghton Mifflin.

Kolozak, K. (2004, July/August). Assessing your center to create a diverse staff. *Exchange*, 55–58.

Kriete, R. (1999). Morning meeting: A powerful way to begin the day. *Responsive Classroom, 11*(1), 1–3.

Langan, P. (2002). *Bullying in schools: What you need to know*. West Berlin, NJ: Townsend Press Book Center.

Levin, D. E. (2003). *Teaching young children in violent times: Building a peaceable classroom* (2nd ed.). Cambridge, MA: Educators for Social Responsibility.

Levine, M. D. (1992). *All kinds of minds*. Cambridge, MA: Educators Publishing Service.

Lubeck, S. (1994). The politics of developmentally appropriate practice. In B. L. Mallory & R. S. New (Eds.), *Diversity and developmentally appropriate practices* (pp. 17–43). New York: Teachers College Press.

Lynch, E. (2000). Developing cross-cultural competence. In E. Lynch & M. Hanson (Eds.), *Developing cross-cultural competence* (pp. 47–89). Baltimore, MD: Paul H. Brooks.

Macintyre, C. (2000). *The art of action research in the classroom*. London: David Fulton.

Mackenzie, R. J. (2003). *Setting limits in the classroom* (Rev. ed.). New York: Three Rivers.

Marland, S. (1972). *Education of the gifted and talented*. Report to the Congress of the United States by the U.S. Commissioner of Education. Washington, DC: U.S. Government Printing Office.

Marzano, R. J. (2003). *Classroom management that works: Research-based strategies for every teacher*. Alexandria, VA: Association for Supervision and Curriculum Development.

Maslow, A. H. (1954). *Motivation and personality*. New York: Harper & Row.

Minde, K. (1998). The sleep of infants and why parents matter. *Zero to Three, 19*(2), 9–14.

Montessori, M. (1965). *Spontaneous activity in education: The advanced Montessori method*. New York: Schocken.

Montessori, M. (1967). *The absorbent mind*. New York: Dell.

National Association for the Education of Young Children. (1990). *Media violence and children*. Washington, DC: Author.

Nelsen, J., Erwin, C., & Duffy, R. (1995). *Positive discipline for preschoolers*. Rocklin, CA: Prima.

Olds, A. (1987). Places of beauty. In D. Bergen (Ed.), *Readings from Play as a medium for learning and development* (pp. 123–127). Olney, MD: Association for Childhood Education International.

Payne, R. (1998). *A framework for understanding poverty*. Baytown, TX: RFT.

Phillips, C. B. (1994). The movement of African-American children through sociocultural contexts. In B. L. Mallory & R. S. New (Eds.), *Diversity and Developmentally Appropriate Practices* (pp. 137–154). New York: Teachers College Press.

Piaget, J. (1926). *Judgment and reasoning in the child*. New York: Harcourt, Brace, and World.

Piaget, J. (1929). *The child's conception of the world* (J. & A. Tomlinson, Trans.). New York: Harcourt, Brace and World.

Piaget, J. (1954). *The construction of reality in the child.* New York: Basic Books.

Pollack, W. (1998). *Real boys.* New York: Henry Holt.

Popham, W. J. (2001). *The truth about testing.* Alexandria, VA: Association for Supervision and Curriculum Development.

Rea, L., & Parker, R. (1997). *Designing and conducting survey research: A comprehensive guide.* San Francisco: Jossey-Bass.

Renzulli, J. (1978). What makes giftedness? Reexamining a definition. *Phi Delta Kappan, 60,* 180–184, 261.

Ritchie, J. (2001). Reflections on collectivism in early childhood teaching in Aotearoa/New Zealand. In S. Grieshaber & G. S. Cannella (Eds.), *Embracing identities in early childhood education: Diversity and possibilities* (pp. 133–147). New York: Teachers College Press.

Ross, P. O. (1993). *National excellence: A case for developing America's talent.* Washington, DC: U.S. Government Printing Office.

Seefeldt, C. (1998). Assessing young children. In C. Seefeldt (Ed.), *Continuing issues in early childhood education* (pp. 314–338). Columbus, Ohio: Merrill.

Seeley, K. R. (1993). Gifted students at risk. In L. K. Silverman (Ed.), *Counseling the gifted and talented* (pp. 263–276). Denver: Love.

Seeman, H. (2000). *Preventing classroom discipline problems* (3rd ed.). Landham, MD: Scarecrow Press.

Seigle, P., Lange, L., & Macklem, G. (2003). *Open circle program.* Wellesley, MA: Stone Center, Wellesley College.

Short-Camilli, C. (1994). *Bullyproofing your school: A comprehensive approach for elementary schools.* Longmont, CO: Sopris West.

Simmons, R. (2002). *Odd girl out: The hidden culture of aggression in girls.* New York: Harcourt.

Sisk, D. (1987). *Creative teaching of the gifted.* New York: McGraw-Hill.

Spock, B., & Rothenberg, M. B. (1985). *Dr. Spock's baby and child care.* New York: Pocket Books.

Springate, K. W., & Stegelin, D. A. (1999). *Building school and community partnerships through parent involvement.* Upper Saddle River, NJ: Prentice-Hall.

Steyer, J. P. (2002). *The other parent.* New York: Atria Books.

Stone, J. G. (2001). *Building a classroom community: The early childhood teacher's role.* Washington, DC: National Association for the Education of Young Children.

Subrahmanyam, K., Kraut, R., Greenfield, P., & Gross, E. (2001). New forms of electronic media. In D. G. Singer & J. L. Singer (Eds.), *Handbook of children and the media* (pp. 395–414). Thousand Oaks, CA: Sage.

Terman, L. (1925). Mental and physical traits of a thousand gifted children. In L. Terman (Ed.), *Genetic studies of genius* (Vol. 1). Stanford, CA: Stanford University.

Thomas, A., & Chess, S. (1996). *Temperament: Theory and practice.* New York: Brunner/Mazel.

Thompson, K. (2001). Violence in E-rated video games. *Journal of the American Medical Association, 286,* 591–598.

Thompson, M., & Grace, C. O. (2001). *Best friends, worst enemies.* New York: Ballantine.

Tomlinson, C. A. (1999). *The differentiated classroom: Responding to the needs of all learners.* Alexandria, VA: Association for Supervision and Curriculum Development.

Tomlinson, C. A. (2001). *How to differentiate instruction in mixed-ability classrooms.* Alexandria, VA: Association for Supervision and Curriculum Development.

Tomlinson, C. A. (2003). *Fulfilling the promise of the differentiated classroom.* Alexandria, VA: Association for Supervision and Curriculum Development.

Twenge, J. (2000). The age of anxiety? Birth cohort change in anxiety and neuroticism. *Journal of Personality and Social Psychology, 79,* 1007–1021.

University of the State of New York, State Education Department. (n.d.). *English language arts resource guide with core curriculum.* Albany, Author.

Velting, O. N., Setzer, N. J., & Albano, A. M. (2002). Anxiety disorders. In D. T. Marsch & M. A. Fristad (Eds.), *Handbook of serious emotional disturbance in children and adolescents* (pp. 204–227). New York: John Wiley & Sons.

Vygotsky, L. S. (1978). *Mind in society.* Cambridge, MA: Harvard University Press.

Washington, V., & Andrews, J. D. (Eds.). (1998). *Children of 2010.* Washington, DC: National Association for the Education of Young Children.

Westberg, K. L., Burns, D. E., Gubbins, E. J., Reis, S. M., Park, S., & Maxfield, L. R. (1998). *Development practices in gifted education: Results of a national survey.* Storrs, CT: University of Connecticut National Research Center on Gifted and Talented.

Whitehead, B. D. (1993, April). Dan Quayle was right. *Atlantic Monthly, 271*(4), 47–84.

Whitemore, J. (1980). *Giftedness, conflict, and underachievement.* Boston: Allyn & Bacon.

Willis, W. (1996). Families with African American Roots. In E. W. Lynch & M. J. Hanson (Eds.), *Developing cross-cultural competence* (pp. 165–207). Baltimore: Paul H. Brookes.

Winnicott, D. W. (1987). *Babies and their mother.* Reading, MA: Addison-Wesley.

Wiseman, R. (2002). *Queen bees and wannabes.* New York: Crown.

Witkin, G. (1999). *KidStress.* New York: Penguin Books.

Wood, C. (1997). *Yardsticks: Children in the classroom ages 4–14*. Greenfield, MA: Northeast Foundation for Children.

Wyckoff, J., & Unell, B. C. (1984). *Discipline without shouting or spanking*. Minnetonka, MN: Meadowbrook.

Yang, A., & Charney, R. S. (2005). Buddy teachers. *Responsive Classroom, 17*(1), 1–3.

Zeitlin, S., Williamson, G. G., & Szczepanski, M. (1988). *Early coping inventory: A measure of adaptive behavior*. Bensenville, IL: Scholastic Testing Service.

Index

About the Authors

Dr. **Janet Andron Hoffman** is an educator, teacher-trainer, licensed clinical social worker, and consultant. After practicing psychotherapy and facilitating parenting groups, she earned a doctorate from Teachers College, Columbia University in curriculum and teaching. In addition to her position as an adjunct assistant professor in early childhood education at Teachers College, Dr. Hoffman designs and presents workshops on topics including child development, discipline, emotional intelligence, and balancing work and family life. Dr. Hoffman has been consulting with an inner-city Bronx, New York preschool program that was awarded a federal grant to promote literacy. Currently Dr. Hoffman is serving as a school social worker at the Abraham Joshua Heschel School in New York City. She is married with three children.

Along with a doctorate in curriculum and teaching from Teachers College, Columbia University, Dr. **Eileen Flicker** holds masters degrees in developmental psychology, educational psychology, and early childhood education, as well as teaching and administrative certifications. She has worked as a teacher, childcare director, curriculum coordinator, college professor, program developer, and educational and mental health consultant. Currently Dr. Flicker works in schools where she facilitates differentiated instruction and social skills groups. Dr. Flicker resides in upstate New York with her husband and three children.